Feminist Family Values Forum

Mililani Trask, Gloria Steinem,
Angela Davis, María Jiménez

Presented by the

Foundation for a Compassionate Society

*Produced by Plain View Press in collaboration with the
Foundation for a Compassionate Society.*

Edited by Susan Bright.

Photos © Jane Steig Parsons, Prints Charming Photography

ISBN: 0-911051-86-4
Library of Congress: 96-069454
Copyright The Foundation for a Compassionate Society, 1996.
All Rights Reserved.

Thanks to Sue MacNicholls, Maren Hicks, María Limón, Megan Bright
for proof reading and to Danna Byrom and Jane Steig Parsons for sharing
photo documentation of the forum; to Margo LaGattuta and Mary Hebert
for text editing; and to Sue Littleton for transcribing the conference tapes.
Thanks to Esther Lopez, Diana James, Amy Richards, Ann Long and Renée
Trask for facilitating editing and proof reading with our keynote speakers.

Cover photograph of the Alma de Mujer Conference Retreat Center
provided courtesy of the center. Sculpture from Alma's Meditation Knoll is
from the "Madre del Mundo" series created by Marsha Gómez.

Thanks to Mark Ely for photoshop work on the cover.

Some of the Foundation staff members: Suze Kemper, Francesca Blue Conover, Sally Jacques, Ana
Sisnett, Erin Rogers and María Limón, SanJuanita Alcalá, Yana Bland, Rose Corrales.
Middle photo © Jana Birchum.

Plain View Press
P. O. 33311
Austin, TX 78764
512-441-2452

Foundation for a
Compassionate Society
P.O. Box 868
Kyle, TX 78640
512-447-6222

Available at special 50% bookstore and text book rates from the Foundation
or Plain View Press. Distributed by Baker and Taylor. Audio and Video tapes of
the forum are available from the Foundation for a Compassionate Society.

Contents

Introductions
Lourdes Pérez   4
Sally Jacques   5
Genevieve Vaughan   6

Keynote Speakers

Mililani Trask   11
   Intro: Marsha Goméz   10

María de los Angeles Jiménez   26
   Intro: Patricia Salas   24

Gloria Steinem   42
   Intro: Pat Cuney   40

Angela Davis   57
   Intro: María Limón   56

Dialogue   64

Feminist Family Values Essay
   and Art Contest   **76**

Community Program   78

   Intro: Genevieve Vaughan   77
   Intro: María Limón   80

Community Speakers

   Ana Sisnett   81
   Mary Ellen Curtin   82
   Dottie Curry   83
   Sharon Bridgforth   84
   Lillian Stevens   86
   Dr. Mercedes Lynn
     de Uriarte   87
   Andrea Beckham   90
   Stephanie Thomas   90

D'An Anders   92
Anna Belle Burleson   93
Moira Dolan   94
Candra Gaither   95
Carol Joseph   96
Shakti Miller   97
Jude Filler   98
Melissa Garcia   99
Sonia Inge   100
Marta Cotera   100
Elizabeth Fernea   102
Tammy Goméz   103
Yana Bland   105
Sylvia Herrera   107
María Loya   108
Susana Almanza   109
Any Wong Mok   110

**What is the Foundation for a
Compassionate Society?**
   by Genevieve Vaughan   112

International Special Projects 122
Facilities   126
Media Projects   128
Anti-Nuclear Projects   130

Sekhmet, the goddess of the
Temple near the Nuclear Test
site in Nevada. Created by
Marsha Gómez.

Lourdes Peréz

Singer, Songwriter

Homenaje a Gloria Anzaldúa
letra y música por Lourdes Pérez

Te vendieron, me vendieron, el dolor
es pasajero
Manantiales de tus versos quedarán
El bagaje que aquí llevo
Se desprenderá de nuevo
Otra piel que dejo al viento y volará.

(translation)
They sold you, they sold me
The pain will pass
The pond that is your verse
will
remain
The baggage that I carry
will fall
from me once again
Another skin that I leave to
the
wind
And it will fly

Historia escrita en sangre
Sangre color de miel
Traición desierto de hambre
Amargura de hiel

History written in blood
Blood the color of honey
Betrayal, desert of hunger
The bitterness of bile

Los puntos cardinales
Llevo bajo mi tez
Brazos que abarcan mundo
Nueva Raza seré

The cardinal points
I carry under my skin
Arms that embrace the
world
A New Race I will be

El velo del silencio
Cantando morderé
Cambiando mis adentros
Nueva lengua tendré

The veil of silence
Singing, I will bite it
Changing my insides
A New Tongue I will have

Mis manos laboriosas
Amando a otra mujer
Saldré yo victoriosa
Vívora/cascabel

My working hands
Loving another woman
I will emerge victorious
Serpent/snake

Photo © Danna Byrom, 1996.

Sally Jacques

Dancer, Choreographer
Foundation for a Compassionate Society

Words cannot express the excitement, pride, joy and honor the organizing committee feels bringing together this amazing group of people, the speakers, and you, the audience, who are all part of an historical moment.

The speakers tonight are pioneers committed to the issues that move them. They do so in the face of a national backlash against women, and sometimes under threat to their personal safety. Their legacy and courage affect all of our lives. The purpose for our gathering is not to develop a homogenized feminist position, but rather to expand feminist discourse. Before it grows a leaf, a tree sends out an energy matrix. The inspiration, motivation, and greatest wish for this evening is to provide a forum for the kinds of issues and perspectives that are not represented fully in the media.

This forum, coupled with the resource each of us presents in our collective intelligence, passion and commitment to advance the struggle for peace and liberation for all peoples can then move forward the process of clarification of our vision.

This vision, by definition, must be multifaceted and informed by all of our various experiences. We are all trees developing our energy matrices, envisioning our lives as we wish them to be. As we put ourselves in the center of our powerful lives, we effect change all around us to the benefit of everyone and every living thing on the planet.

So thank you for being here, and now I would like to introduce Lourdes Peréz, a jewel Austin inherited from the nation of Puerto Rico.

In November, when Lourdes opened for Mercedes Sosa, she brought the house down with her own passion and commitment to liberation struggles. Welcome!

Photo © Jane Steig Parsons, Prints Charming Photography

Genevieve Vaughan

Founder, Foundation for a Compassionate Society

It's wonderful to see you all here. This event is really a great thing. In celebration of Mother's Day, let me say that we need to invent or find within ourselves a mother-based economic system, that is based on caring for needs, instead of on stimulating greed.

I believe that women are socialized into caring and therefore that we already have an alternative value system within ourselves, which many men also have. I created the Foundation for a Compassionate Society in an attempt to try to put caring values into reality. The Foundation is not a society of particularly compassionate people, rather we are trying to make the society itself compassionate. This momentous task has been made more difficult by right-wing messages and interpretations which are broadcast towards us from all sides, discouraging women from taking the initiative. Yet, most of us know in our hearts that something is terribly wrong, and we welcome the possibility of contributing to social change.

Working together in the Foundation has allowed a diverse group of women to support each other for a vision of a better world. We have been made stronger by the women who have come before us and those who are still contributing their unflagging energy to social change. Now I want to welcome our keynote speakers. I am glad that these almost mythological women have come to share their thinking with us.

I hope we will be inspired by them to think deeply and to act courageously, as all of them have done in their different ways. The staff members of the Foundation have done an excellent job in pulling this conference together. All of them do wonderful work in their various projects. I would like to ask the Foundation staff to stand so that you can applaud them and to give a special thanks to the women who have worked on this event. Foundation staff, stand up, please.

Photo © Jane Steig Parsons, Prints Charming Photography

6

The women who worked on this event particularly are Pat Cuney, Sally Jacques, Suze Kemper, María Limón, Sue MacNicholls, Patty Salas, Erin Rogers, Ana Sisnett, a special hand to all of them—and to Freida Werden and Beth Wichterich who are in charge of the audio and video components for this evening.

I would also like to thank the volunteers for their important help during the preparation and tonight, and thank you all for coming. My hope is that this evening will stimulate a wide scale discussion of values which will liberate all of us from the stereotypical thinking and ideological control of the right wing.

For many years I have been working on a theory of values. Even economists do not know what "value" is, and yet it influences our lives every day. So when the right wing started talking about "family values," I suspected they didn't know what they were talking about, and I knew I wanted to bring women together to discuss our common take on them.

I believe feminists have the first collective philosophy, and that we are putting it together from all our different points of view. By uniting with each other across all the boundaries patriarchy creates, we can finally step back from the brink of human and planetary disaster. We need to create widespread social change. We think too much within our own system, and not outside of it. The personal and the political are one, but taking personal power without taking political power leaves the system unscathed and allows it to adapt superficially without creating those large scale, systemic changes which are necessary for the survival of the planet.

For example, as Rosalie Bertell says, we may stop using underarm deodorant, but if we do not stop the Air Force jet flights, the hole in the ozone will continue to grow, because the jets are many times more damaging than the all the spray cans on earth. Our government keeps us ignorant of the damage done by Air Force jets. We mistakenly believe that by changing only our individual lives (stopping using spray cans for instance), we are making the difference. We have to liberate ourselves from our ignorance and take our power to make the changes in a system which is dispowering our hearts and creating a context of scarcity which makes caring impractical and even self-sacrificial.

Taking political power without recognizing women's values, our values, as specifically different, also leaves the system unscathed. Margaret Thatcher is the example that is usually given for this kind of success. Our capitalist system espouses the values of hierarchy and competition, which are usually considered the values of patriarchy. Individualism, when it is seen as the philosophy of every man for himself, is also a position of capitalism.

In other words, patriarchal capitalism has the ego-oriented values that feminists oppose in the individual men and in our lives. Behind the mask of fair and free market, in the big picture, the system itself has a perpetrator's face. Patriarchy is a collective psychosis; it functions on many different levels, like a fractal self-similar image. It hurts men and women, and creates dominant classes and races. In the big picture, the countries of the North practice the patriarchal family values of domination and submission on the countries of the South, making those of us in the so-called "First World" accomplices of our country's policies, whether or not we reap the benefits directly.

There is no improvement in our individual situations as feminists in the First World that can change our belonging to this perpetrators' society. We have to take our efforts and energy, our alternative values, outside of our homes and private lives, into the arena in which large scale policies are decided. The patriarchal values only recreate the problems again and again, at different levels.

Structurally, my own position as a wealthy woman who has many advantages, is similar to the position of the U.S. with regard to Third World countries. Unless I, or unless all of us think and act beyond the boundaries of privileged categories, class or race, or nation or sex, we are parts of the perpetrator system, causing the suffering of millions of people and the devastation of the planet. We have to pose the problem to ourselves and act to change this system from within, and there is no way out of it, no space on the planet where we can be inactive and innocent.

I believe that the macho ego, whether it belongs to an individual or to a nation, is a social product which is an aberration, not the norm, and that the values of care which are still being practiced mostly by women in this society, are the normal way of behaving for all. The values of care are not incorporated into the social structures. Look, for example, at aid to Third World countries, which is said to be a gift, but is actually a hidden exchange. This travesty disqualifies caring and makes it seem unrealistic. Reality itself is made to be patriarchal. Values motivate systems; women's values could motivate a completely different kind of system from the one we have now. The right wing, patriarchal values have never solved the problems they and their system have created. We have to think and act together quickly to create a new system and a new reality now. Thank you.

Photo © Jane Steig Parsons, Prints Charming Photography

Marsha Gómez

Director, Alma de Mujer

I am a mother, and one of the co-founding mothers and board members of the Indigenous Women's Network, director of Alma de Mujer Center for Social Change, which has been a project of the Foundation for a Compassionate Society for the past eight years, and which has recently been transferred and made a gift from Genevieve to the Indigenous Women's Network.

It is my honor tonight to introduce to you one of my heroes, *comadre*, and sister board member of the Indigenous Women's Network. Mililani Trask is *"Kia'aina"* of her Nation. *"Kia'aina"* is the head of the state of Ka Lahui, which is the sovereign native Hawai'ian nation, which has a citizenry of approximately twenty-five thousand native Hawai'ian people.

Attorney at Law, Mililani has dedicated her skills and her practice, literally, her heart, body and soul to the self-determination of her people and the protection of the land base there. She has litigated endlessly, tirelessly, head-on with corporate, multi-national adversaries. She has protected sacred sites, has won back homelands for her people. Her work has led her to international commissions, initiatives and conferences where she has served a major leadership role with indigenous nations and people of color. She has recently worked on the indigenous peace initiative with Rigoberta Menchu-Tum and the U.N.P.O., the Unrecognized Nations and Peoples Organizations, founded by the Dalai Lama in 1991. She returned from D.C. yesterday, where she sits on a board with the environmental and economic justice globalization think-tank.

It is with utmost respect and honor I introduce Mililani Trask.

Photo © Rita DeBellis.

Mililani Trask

Kanaka, Nation of Ka Lahui Hawai'i

It's a great honor and pleasure for me to participate in this most distinguished panel on behalf of the Nation of Ka Lahui Hawai'i, as a member of the Indigenous Women's Network, as an ambassador in the Indigenous Initiative for Peace, and (for) our sister, Rigoberta Menchu-Tum, and also on behalf of the Unrepresented Nations and People's Organization founded in 1991 by His Holiness the Dalai

Lama for those nations who are not recognized or given a seat in the United Nations.

Several months ago, I was busy at my desk and received a telephone call. At the time I wasn't taking calls, so my secretary Renée came in and said, "Mililani, there's someone on the phone, and I know you'll want to speak with her; it's Genevieve Vaughan." I told her I always have time for Gen and got on the phone.

"Mililani," Gen said, "we're putting together something that's going to be a watershed event for the women's agenda in the coming decade. It will be in Austin, Texas." She explained what her goals were, and why the Foundation for a Compassionate Society had committed itself to this great undertaking. She honored me and invited me to come. I told her I'd be there and promptly forgot about it. Several weeks later, Renée came into my office and showed me the faxes that had come regarding my speaking engagement on Feminist Family Values. I told Renée that it must be a mistake, because I would never agree to speak at a gathering on Feminist Family Values.

Looking at the papers, I thought this could mean two things: either that feminists are coming together to talk about family values, values for their children, their daughters and sons, values to use in their families with their husbands, or, that the feminist family is coming together to talk about their values as feminists. In either case, I knew I wasn't supposed to be speaking, since I don't have a husband and never have; I don't have children that I've given birth to, so in the dominant social sense I don't have a nuclear family.

Furthermore, I'm not a feminist. I've never considered myself to be a feminist. I've always believed that feminists were white women with positions of stature and money, and other such things, which clearly I am not. So I looked at the papers and listened to Renée saying, "No, you confirmed this, this is what Gen called you about," and I thought, "Darn that Gen! Is she throwing me another curve ball?" Taking a closer look, I saw that in the typical Gen Vaughan style, she had given us a title that is controversial, and in so doing, invited us to accept the challenge of change.

So I've traveled a great distance to address women's political agendas for the coming decade, to discuss women's empowerment, and to present for your consideration and review two things: The first is the Beijing Declaration of the Indigenous Women who gathered in August of 1995 to prepare their own agenda for the coming decade; the second is to bring forward the Beijing Challenge that was issued from Beijing, a challenge to expand feminist thought on the issue of gender equity.

I believe we are prepared for this debate. I want to begin by reviewing the great products, of which I am still proud, which came out of the indigenous women's tent in Beijing. Beijing was a great, great undertaking, and was possibly one of the most important events in my life. Logistically, it was a mess. 35,000 women came, and we were only the ones who made it! Nearly 20,000 more women did not make it to Beijing because the oppressive government of China would not issue them visas.

When we arrived in Beijing, the oppressive, paternalistic government of China had girded its loins for thousands of women, coming from all over the world, to burn their bras. I'm not joking. In the taxicabs of Huairou and Beijing were folded up old military blankets to be thrown on us the moment we bared our breasts and burned our bras. I was laughing with Gen about this, and speaking with Gloria Steinem about this impression placed in the minds of these Chinese leaders, that women were coming there to burn their bras. Then I got to wondering whether that ever actually happened. Thanks to Gen and Gloria, I now know the true story. There never were any bras burned at the Miss America pageant so many years ago because they couldn't get a fire permit.

So while we corrected a great misunderstanding in the minds of the male leaders of China, we also struck a blow for what was really women's empowerment. I don't like the label feminism; I've always felt that it had certain racial and socio-economic connotations, as Gen Vaughan has pointed out. Yet as I criticize this term and challenge us all to stop using it, and to start speaking in terms of women's empowerment and women's agendas, I also want to acknowledge that we have all been victimized by negative connotations which have been cultivated by the white male-dominated media of the West.

Many women from all over the world met in Beijing. There were so many events that it was impossible to participate in everything. It was a great blessing for all of us that the Cordillero women from the Philippines had the foresight and resources to put together an indigenous women's tent, and there for twelve days and nights, indigenous women of the world came. We overcame racial barriers, cultural divisions, and economic gaps, to write a joint global statement that has subsequently been printed in many different languages.

In talking about this statement, I encourage you all to take the time to read and reflect upon it, because it contains the *"mana,"* the thought of the indigenous women's global movement. Since our gathering has occurred on Mother's Day, it begins appropriately:

"The earth is our mother; from her we receive our life and our ability to live. It is our responsibility to care for our mother, and in caring for our mother, we care for ourselves. Women, all females, are a manifestation of Mother Earth in human form. We stand in unity behind this 1995 'Beijing Declaration of Indigenous Women,' which is the fruit of our collective efforts to understand the world and our situation as indigenous women, to critique the draft platform for action, and articulate our demands to the international community, the governments of the world, and the NGOs. The new world order, which is engineered by those who have abused and raped Mother Earth, colonized, marginalized and discriminated against us, is being imposed upon us viciously. This is re-colonization coming under the name of globalization and trade liberalization. The forces behind this are the rich industrialized nation states, the transnational corporations, and the financial institutions which they control, like the World Bank, the International Monetary Fund, and the World Trade Organizations. They will cooperate and compete among themselves to the last frontiers of the earth's natural resources, located on our traditional land."

That is the beginning statement of the Indigenous Women's Global Declaration that issued from Beijing. I'd like to discuss some of the more important parts of this Declaration, and begin by sharing a bit of the history of my people.

I am Kanaka Maoli; I am native Hawai'ian. Hawai'i is the north easternmost area of the archipelagos of the Pacific Basin. The Pacific Basin is the largest region in the world, which few people realize. This is not taught in the schools, because we are island

14

people, and what dominates our education is Western continental thought. Many people also don't know that, until 1893, Hawai'i was an independent nation. We are considered to be the oldest indigenous nation in the world that was able to come abreast of more enlightened Western colonization.

In 1778 Hawai'i was allegedly discovered by Captain James Cook, the imperializing Britisher, who sailed from Europe and declared that he discovered Hawai'i for the Europeans, and for the English, specifically. When he landed upon our shores there were one million people living in a matrilineal society; yet he promptly declared that we belonged to Britain. The British sphere of influence ended when American sugar planters came with their own economic plan. In 1893, United States Marine gunboats sailed into Honolulu Harbor, dispersed their implements of death and destruction, the cannon and the musket, and overthrew our queen. At the time of the United States overthrow, we had in place twenty-two international covenants and conventions of friendship and recognition with all of the enlightened Western nations of the world. We had treaties of friendship and peace with France and Britain, Germany, Switzerland, Imperial Japan and others; and several treaties with the United States, but we now see, historically, the emptiness of those words.

Thus we were colonized and imperialized in 1893; our kingdom overthrown. A puppet government, installed for five years, was run by a man named Stanford B. Dole. While few may know him, I'm sure everyone, in one way or another, has consumed his products: Dole pineapple. He was the man whom the President of the United States put in power over our independent nation. When Cook arrived there were one million Kanaka Maoli; a generation and a half later, at the time of the United States overthrow, 39,000 of us remained. Today we are 200,000 Kanaka Maoli. You see that our population is increasing, because we love each other.

There is a saying in the Hawai'ian culture that you can marry whomever you wish, but mate with your own kind. In this way, we regenerate our numbers. We had a matrilineal society, which does not mean that men were marginalized or oppressed, but that women played essential roles, not only in governing and land tenure, but also in the spiritual realm. In matrilineal societies, such as Hawai'i, it is my brothers who would teach my sons the ways of fishing and gathering and hunting. In matrilineal societies, women are not marginalized, nor are we given easy outs in difficult times. For instance, during times of war in most societies, women would take the children and the elders and flee to the mountains, while in Hawai'i, the elders took the children to the mountains and the women took their spears to the battlefield with the men.

When we gathered in Beijing, it was heartening to see representatives from matrilineal societies, because there are very few of us remaining, most of whom, in my estimation, are indigenous cultures. After looking at the global agenda, struggling with it day and night for twelve days, we divided our statement into six areas, the first being a critique of the Beijing platform of action.

I don't want to diminish the work that the United Nations has accomplished in Beijing. Many of the points on the Beijing platform of action, adopted by the United Nations, are important. There were, however, significant omissions and deficiencies. Primarily, the Beijing platform was not critical of, nor did it analyze, what is now known as the New World Order. It failed to examine the impact of transnational corporations and their international financiers. It did not consider the root causes of poverty among women. It did not address, with any integrity, the economic basis for the poverty of women globally, because it could not: because the creators of the platform were blinded by the agendas of the American and European transnational corporations and their international financiers.

It is for this reason that addressing and analyzing the New World Order, also known as globalization—the expansion of transnationals, and their voracious appetite for consuming the natural and human resources of the world—is the primary agenda of the global indigenous women's community, who comprise the majority of the women of the world.

The majority of the women of the world are women of color and indigenous women. We are the ones who live under poverty; we are the ones who suffer at the hands of militarism, and from violence in all forms, and our suffering is at a greater rate than others. 70% of the world peoples who live in tragic situations of poverty today are women. Women are viewed by transnational corporations not as human beings, but as cheap sources of labor. We need to understand this; we need to confront this; we need to enunciate this. We need to stand up to this pattern of globalization and realize that when we see it with our women's eye, this is a manifestation of paternalism, of colonization, and imperialism. Globalization and the New World Order is the natural consequence of capitalist, paternalistic societies. We need to see this. We need to name it and call it by its rightful name. We need to see that poverty is the result of this, and not the result of anything else. We need to clear the agenda, and be clear in our minds about this.

One of the major issues that we addressed in our Declaration was the expansion of militarism. Militarism is a tool of oppression, a tool that is used against women, and there is a relationship that we see in the global arena with our indigenous eye, between militarism and rape and sexual slavery—the sexual trafficking of indigenous women. Military regimes have used rape as a mechanism to subvert indigenous cultures. Rape is not only a crime that occurs on the streets of the United States; rape is a vehicle of militarism. We must also understand and appreciate the relationship between militarism and the dramatic increase in AIDS and HIV, which is occurring globally in indigenous communities. This is because military forces, whether Americans in Okinawa or others elsewhere in the world, are usually males whose needs to satisfy their sexual drive are indiscriminate. We need to know how this impacts the spread of AIDS and HIV in our world communities. While many express concern about AIDS and HIV in the context of personal health and prevention, few seem to address with any integrity the relationship between militarism and the spread of AIDS globally. We must address this issue if we are going to stop the AIDS-HIV epidemic.

Because of these failures by the program of action issued by the United Nations, the Indigenous Women's global Declaration further set forth their own platform of demands.

The first is to recognize and respect our right to self-determination as women; we are not just the mothers of children, we are also the mothers of nations. We need to enunciate our agenda by asserting our right to self-determination. Our rights are defined in the *"International Covenant of Civil and Political Rights"* as follows:

"The right of self-determination is the right of all peoples, not just men, but all peoples, to determine our political status, and by virtue of this right, to structure our own political futures; to determine and define how we wish to develop our economies, how we wish to utilize our land, and how we wish to create economic programs in our community and structure health care programs. This is the right of self-determination. It is an international human right, and it is time that we enunciate our right as women in terms of international legal standards that for too long have only been applied to white males from the dominant society."

Secondly, we demanded that the nations of the world recognize and respect our right to our territories, lands, and natural resources, and our right for self-development, education and health, in ways that are culturally appropriate to our people. Because we are vitally concerned with developing community-based economic programs and addressing critical health needs, we acknowledge and understand, as women from indigenous societies, that these programs must be culturally appropriate. You cannot take health programs that have been developed in New York down to Haiti, impose them upon the community, then wonder why the programs fail. In order to address the health needs of the women from South Africa, or women from the Philippines, you must first acknowledge those cultures by putting the health program in the appropriate cultural context, if such programs are going to be effective.

The third area we examined was environmental toxicity, and the other side of that ugly little coin— environmental racism. A bad habit of the transnational and G-7 nations is consuming our resources, creating toxic byproducts, then bringing those toxic byproducts back to the lands of indigenous peoples.

The women of Hawai'i have the highest rate of breast cancer in the world because in Hawai'i, for years, there was toxic dumping of DDT, long after America outlawed the use of DDT on the continent. It was prohibited only in the continental United States. Why? To make sure that American companies would have open markets in Cuba, the Philippines, and Hawai'i, to dump it on our lands. So DDT is in our water system. You might think that the highest rate of breast cancer would be somewhere else in the Third World, but it's not. It's in Hawai'i. Toxic dumping, the mining of uranium, and other such demonic practices have a necessary consequence, and that is environmental racism. Where are toxic dumps and nuclear rods being stored? Why are they only on American Indian land, or in the communities of black people and Spanish-speaking Americans? There is a new term we need to learn: "environmental racism." It is one facet of racism.

A fourth area that we debated in Beijing had to do with our rights to cultural and intellectual property, and our rights to control the biological diversity of our territories. The Creator has given us a great blessing, the diversity of the earth, and the diversity of all of the life forms of the earth. This is our cultural heritage. All indigenous women know that we're placed here to be guardians of the sacred Earth, our mother. We are her daughters; that is our calling, that is our place. We know this from the time of our birth, and even before, in our mother's womb. We are indigenous. When we are born, that is when we are called American. Nationality is only a sign based on the geography of where we are born, but before that time, in our mother's womb, we are indigenous women.

Now, however, American and European pharmaceutical companies have embarked upon the copyrighting of life forms. They are taking leaves and trees; they are taking animals; they are registering them. They are saying, "We own this, and because we, as a pharmaceutical, own this leaf, you cannot use it for healing. You cannot make medicine from it, you cannot cure cancer with it, unless you pay us." The Bio-diversity Convention was passed in Rio. Many of us wept at that time. They said that we should celebrate, because now there were finally going to be international laws and rules in place to protect the rights of indigenous peoples, to insure that we would benefit from the great wealth of bio-diversity given to us by the Creator, our Mother. I was one of those who wept, because life forms shouldn't be owned by American pharmaceuticals. There is something demonic about that.

If you think that this is the most outrageous and insidious thing you've ever heard, this is only the first step. American pharmaceuticals and scientific communities, and their supporters at the United Nations, have also determined that within the next fifty to one hundred years, there will be certain cultures of indigenous peoples that will pass away as a result of the scientific communities' own ethnicidal and genocidal practices. Seven hundred indigenous cultures are slated for extinction in the coming hundred years. These pharmaceutical companies are very worried, because they now realize that incorporated in our genetic material are traits that they do not have in the dominant society. So they have created a new program called the Human Genome Project. The Human Genome Project is gathering the hair, skin and blood of the seven hundred indigenous cultures of the world who are set for extinction and putting these genetic materials in the deep freeze. They want the blood and the hair of the Eskimos, because Eskimos can survive extreme low temperatures, and are healthy and strong without eating vegetables. This would be a powerful factor for a nation's military, having this trait. So before the Eskimos vanish, the pharmaceuticals think, we had better get their blood and hair.

Who's on the list? Indigenous peoples in the Pacific Basin are; we from Hawai'i are on the list. So, indigenous peoples in Central and South America, Africa, and Asia had better check the list, find out about the Human Genome Project, and join your indigenous sisters in stopping this little diabolical plan.

There in Beijing, we were so outraged, we marched over to the World Health Organization and shut down the funding plan for the Human Genome Project, right then and there! "Gentlemen," I told them, " you may be surprised to learn that your plan for genocide of my people will not work. That's what you thought when you sent the military gunboats in 1893, you got us close to extinction at 39,000. But in the last hundred or so years, our numbers are coming back, and we don't intend to let them fall any further."

Among the work that came out of Beijing is the challenge issued by indigenous women and women of color to the feminist global community to expand feminist thinking regarding the issue of gender equity. One of the agendas, which the indigenous women of the world objected to surfaced in Cairo when we got bogged down on this issue of gender equity, which was articulated in terms of abortion.

What ultimately happened in Cairo was that all of the women of the Arab world lined up behind the *mullahs*, all of the women of the Christian world, Catholic and Protestant, lined up behind the Vatican; and all of the women of the feminist world lined up behind Bill Clinton, and thus were the issues of abortion and gender equity addressed.

The women of the world cannot align themselves with the dominant patriarchies of the world. We cannot do that. This is the challenge, then, to feminist thought: the indigenous women and women of color that gathered in Beijing do not think that the issue of gender equity should be enunciated as the primary issue.

When we introduced this issue at the beginning of our dialogue, we broke it out according to the perspectives of women of color and indigenous women, and the perspectives of dominant culture, white feminist movements. Many women asked me, "Why make a distinction between women of color and indigenous women?" The answer is that women of color and indigenous women are not the same. Women of color are women of color. They're black women, brown women, red women, they're our sisters from Asia. Indigenous women, however, are not just women of color, but are white women too. Twenty years ago the indigenous women's global movement took on the issue of our own racism and struggled through it. If we can do it, so can everyone else.

Let me tell you a story, lest you think that an indigenous woman leader and a woman who works with Rigoberta Menchu-Tum is somehow immune from racism. I am not. As an indigenous woman I've always believed that indigenous women were women of color. Then, in 1989, I received an invitation to go to Norway, for a global indigenous women's gathering where I was invited to chair the global plenary. It took me days to get there and when I arrived I was suffering from jet lag. I had been told I would be picked up at the airport and when I got off the plane, there were about a hundred people at the airport, but little by little, people got their bags and left. Pretty soon, the only people left at the airport were me and a group of white women, who were wearing beautiful costumes. We looked at each other and they asked me, "Are you Mililani Trask, the Kanaka of Ka Lahui, of Hawai'i?" I said I was and they said, "We're the Sami Women's Delegation—the indigenous women who are hosting the conference." I looked at them, and said, "You're white!" These women had blonde hair, blue eyes, green eyes, and skin so pale it looked like marble.

We struggled and worked together, and by the time I left Norway, I had learned a great lesson about my own racism; that indigenous cultures are not just cultures of color. Indigenous cultures are also white, and I am proud to say, I now have many indigenous sisters who are white sisters. I embrace them; they strengthen me.

What we're saying about the gender equity issue then, is that it's time to stop enunciating gender equity as the primary issue and speak in terms of the empowerment of women and the right of women to self-determination. The gender equity issue is too narrow because it fails to address the issue of racism, economic disparity, and cultural difference. We need to move beyond this, because gender equity supports the dominant culture's paternalistic values.

In Beijing, I got into a debate with several white feminists from America and Canada who still insisted, "Gender equity is the way we have to look at it. You folks say we haven't made any progress, but we have." They proceeded to show me a paper, of which they had made thirty thousand copies, which listed corporate, transnational boards. On this list they noted, since the 1960s, how many seats on these corporate boards had been won by women. My reply to them was, "It is not our goal to have an equal share of chairs in the corporate board rooms of America. It is our goal to change the underlying basis of those corporations." One of the problems that gender equity perpetuates is that it preserves the dominant patrilineal paradigms, which are exactly what we need to change.

The final problem that gender equity presents is that it marginalizes our sisters who are not heterosexual. I'm pleased to say that issue was clarified thanks to the *two-spirit* sisters in Beijing who called the heterosexual sisters on the line, "Excuse me, sisters," they said, " but you have missed one of the fundamental criticisms of the gender equity issue, and that is, the gender equity analysis is heterosexual, and does not address our *two-spirit* issue." *Two-spirit* is a Native American Indian term for those who have different sexual orientation; the Pacific Basin term is *Mahu*. We took a good look at the statement and said, "Thank you, our sisters, for correcting us." Let's admit that, and work on that.

I encourage everyone to examine the indigenous women's statement from Beijing in detail, for it is much more comprehensive than what I have presented here. I invite you to engage in this debate, in this dialogue. I've spoken with many women of color, indigenous women, who doubt that we are ready for this debate, who worry that it could fractionalize the women's movement. The good news, my sisters, is the debate is already happening, and on the forefront are organizations such as the Foundation for Compassionate Society, Bella Abzug and the women in New York who have worked with us many years on the road to Beijing. If you have any trepidation in your heart, you have only to see in this gathering that we have already begun this dialogue. We are capable of this. It is time to move beyond the male media stereotype of feminism and transform this movement into a global movement. There's only one way to do that, and that is by being inclusive on all issues—economic, racial, environmental—that impact the lives of women of color and indigenous women of the world.

We all have a common goal; we know this in our hearts—to make a more compassionate society, for our children, for our sons and daughters, for future generations; a more compassionate society for the earth. This work is a great undertaking. I consider it to be a sacred calling. This work for the earth cannot proceed unless we, each and every one of us, support it.

Photo © Danna Byrom, 1996.

Patricia Salas

Foundation for a Compassionate Society
Board Member, People Organized in Defense of
Earth and Her Resources (PODER)

In 1991 after studying in El Paso to become a midwife, I returned to Austin. At that time, Genevieve Vaughan brought me into the Foundation for a Compassionate Society and asked me to work in Brownsville, to develop a project called Casa de Colores, located on the banks of the Rio Grande River, downstream from Brownsville and Matamoros. About a month after I arrived, I received a visit from two agents of the Border Patrol. Curiously enough, these agents did not come during regular hours. It was well after dark when they knocked on our door. Under the pretense of a "friendly visit," they tried to instill in me a fear of my own people. They told us that when the men on the other side found out that there were two women in this house so close to the river, they would come here and rape us. I immediately thought, however, that it was those two agents who might rape us, and make it look as though it were the work of the men from the other side.

In less than six months of living and working at Casa de Colores, I witnessed many horrors—the dead bodies of Mexican people from the other side—being pulled from the Rio Grande. At any hour of the day or night, agents from the Immigration Service and Drug Enforcement, or local law enforcement officers would arrive and swarm the property to investigate reports of drug crossings, of people crossings, or to pull out murder victims buried on the river's banks. The only person I knew in Texas during this difficult time, to whom I could to reach out for support, was María Jiménez.

I am a documented Mexican, I was born in Texas. The heartache and the harassment that I have experienced in my lifetime—the verbal humiliation, strip-searching—are nothing to the terror suffered by my undocumented, native people: torture and murder at the hands of United States Border Patrol agents.

Photo © Danna Byrom, 1996.

For her tireless work on behalf of our people, which is helping to stop that terror, I am personally grateful to María Jiménez. Her continuing efforts on behalf of human dignity and equality make her work important to us all.

María de los Angeles Jiménez has been the director of the Immigration Law Enforcement Monitoring Project of the American Friends Service Committee for nearly ten years. A working mother, she has been a labor organizer, a human rights activist and has worked for rural development in Mexico. She is currently a member of the Women's Committee of the National Commission for Democracy in México, the official U.S. representative organization for México's Ejercito Zapatista de Liberacion Nacional (EZLN), founded in Chiapas in 1994, to advocate the rights of indigenous peoples.

Photo © Jane Steig Parsons, Prints Charming Photography

María de los Angeles Jiménez

American Friends Service Committee
National Commissin for Democracy in Mexico, Women's Committee

When I was invited to contribute to this forum, I was genuinely surprised, because of all the participants, I am probably the least known. I also realize, however, that I have been asked to participate precisely because what I have to share are the experiences of "unknown" women like myself—women who are faceless, women who struggle, and in their struggle claim dignity not only for themselves, but also for their families and communities.

For many of us who are of Mexican origin, it is very meaningful that this forum on Feminist Family Values occurs on May 10, *"Dia*

Photo © Danna Byrom, 1996.

de las Madres," Mexican Mother's Day. Mother's Day, of course, is the day we recognize the significance of the women who have given us life, nurtured us, taught us, castigated us, reassured us, motivated us and fully impressed upon us our concept of who we are, or who we are not.

The concept of motherhood has long defined us as women in the Mexican culture, although with ambivalence. The concept of motherhood in Mexican culture has symbolically been characterized by two opposites, a duality often expressed by two symbols —the Virgin of Guadalupe on one extreme and the *Llorona* on the other. First, by the symbol of the Virgin of Guadalupe, *"un madre pura,"* a pure mother through whom God is represented, and second, by *"La Llorona,"* the mother who kills her children as an act of vengeance for having been wronged by the man she loves. Either way, we are defined as mothers.

Mexican culture looks upon the mother as a creator of life, not only biologically, but socially, who, by nurturing and building her family, builds the life of the community around her. For most Latinas, a woman and her activities play a central role in developing the family. Likewise, as people of Mexican descent, our lives are shaped by that concept of family, *la familia*, and the central role that mothers play. Consequently, for Latinos in particular, the issue of culture brings many contradictions. In the context of our cultural traditions, fighting for women's rights, for personal independence and dignity is a definitive challenge to the patriarchal system that has bound us.

I remember being about nineteen years old, when I wrote my first article enunciating the right of women to participate fully as citizens, politically and socially. I remember, too, the reaction of my fellow activists—Chicano males—who criticized me. They told me that the abandonment of the family and the traditions we were fighting for was Gringo culture, that I was being brainwashed by white ideology.

Growing up in the United States as I did, as a Mexican immigrant in the sixties, meant surviving discrimination against Mexicans, and confronting anti-Mexican attitudes that both segregated and institutionalized segregation for my compatriots and me. We saw clearly that the only way we would overcome such discrimination, and the second-class citizenship that came with it in Texas and elsewhere in the Southwest, was through our collective actions: actions that would bring an end to this discrimination, and at the same time, transform the society around us.

We became part of a broad civil rights movement called the Chicano Movement, made up of many generations of Mexican Americans who felt that the rest of America had continually questioned our right to be here, and with it our right to belong, to actively participate in the workings of this country. In thinking about the issue of feminism and family values, of "traditional" culture, and the conflicts and tensions that we face as women struggling to integrate these areas, I recall the early years of that Chicano Movement.

My response was to look back—back to the history of Mexico. To remember, as a child, learning about "Sor" (Sister) Juana Inez de la Cruz, the nun who, in 1691, was the first to advocate, in writing, women's right to education, to participate fully in society and develop their human potential. I remember Josefa Ortiz de Dominguez, "La Corregidora," the Mexican equivalent of Paul Revere, who, when the Mexican insurgents were discovered by the Spanish, rode on her horse to alert the people that it was time to rise up against the conquerors.

I remember reading about the women activists of the 1850s, who campaigned for women's education and parity with males in Mexico, particularly in the urban areas of Guadalajara and Mexico City. There was the unforgettable Carmen Domínguez of the family Aquiles de Serdán, who died as a conspirator in the early years of the Mexican Revolution, and the women of Yucatán, who held several feminist congresses to adopt women's equality as part of the new Constitution of 1917. I also remember those who fought for Mexican women's right to vote, which became law in 1953.

These are the facts I rattled off to my fellow Chicano activists nearly three decades ago, telling them finally, "I don't know where your history comes from, but my history, the history of the people of Mexico, is the history of women fighting for their right to participate equally in the economic, political, and social systems of our country. That is my history."

These contradictions between the position of women culturally and the social movements to transform those aspects of gender roles into ones of equality are ever present for Latinas. I remember that one of the earliest obstacles I faced upon my return to Mexico to live in the mid-1970s, was a linguistic one. I had grown accustomed to the feminization of many English words, such as the use of "Congress Person," for "Congressman" and to the ideology behind those early changes. The reality of the Spanish language, however, is such that similar changes in Spanish were not possible because they would alter the basic structure of the language. In accepting the limitations inherent in our language, I began to understand more fully the extent of the struggle faced by Latin American women.

It is striking, for instance, that "*Sor*" Juana Inez de la Cruz, a woman of such intelligence, was questioned by the wisest of men to prove her inferiority, but instead she proved her superiority. It is also significant that when she failed to learn a lesson, she would punish herself by cutting her hair, because the hair was one of the most significant cultural symbols for women during that time. These examples depict the same dilemma faced by Latina feminists: how do we express ourselves with dignity, and at the same time, attempt to rescue and reconnect to our culture and our community?

In looking at the feminist movements in Mexico and the U.S. overall, there is not much difference between them in substance. Both movements work toward women's equality and dignity. In the United States, many Mexican women too have fought for women's equality historically. In this half century like in other periods, the American feminist movement is not monolithic, but is composed of women from diverse backgrounds and groups who work for this single goal, in local communities or nationally, wherever they have landed in the struggle. Thus, the differences are manifested in the form these struggles take. Their expression is confined in spaces defined mostly by the historical moments and socio-economic positions of the women involved. In the Latino experience, women's fight for equality and respect has been profoundly based on the relationship to the family or "*la familia*." "*La familia*" is understood, not only as blood relationship, but as the extended community carved from the cultural concepts of the "*compadres*" and "*comadres*" or co-parents. In that sense, family relationships are valued as essential to our connectedness to community, and our individual well-being to the well-being of our community.

One of the most poignant and moving struggles that illustrate this paradigm in Latin American history is the struggle of the Mothers of the Disappeared which sprang up in the late 1960s to the present. Groups like the Mothers of the Plaza de Mayo in Argentina, COMADRES in El Salvador, the Mutual Support Group of Guatemala, and EUREKA in Mexico were formed in response to the government's secret execution of relatives targeted for their political opposition and activism. They did so, not to assert their prominence in the male power structure, but to assert their moral right as life-givers, as mothers.

To my mind, this movement of the Mothers of the Disappeared was the forerunner of all modern movements seeking democracy throughout Latin America. More significantly, it is this movement that redefined for me the essence of the women's movement. While this is the common vision of women throughout Latin America, for me, a Mexican American living in the United States, this was a new perspective: this courageous campaign against totalitarianism broadened my vision of how women could achieve equality.

In the words of Guadalupe, a member of CONVIGUA (National Coordinator of the Widows of Guatemala): "We did not know what to do after the massacre of 1982. We didn't cook, we didn't eat; our children cried from hunger and pain, but we came to realize that we were left to carry the full responsibility of our family, to feed our children, apart from the great burden of suffering, which we carry around in our hearts." A woman named Teresa, from the Federation of Popular Neighborhoods in Guadalajara, said, "For the woman, the house is hers, and things such as no light and no water are part of the home. So it is her fight."

In this movement, women assert their moral authority as mothers and raise their voices for the the political systems they want and against oppression. Their reproductive and nurturing roles were transformed from the private to the public, the biological to the political. Said a widow in Guatemala: "The first thing we had to conquer was our own fear."

These groups challenged totalitarian regimes and the use of state-initiated violence to suppress the political freedoms of expression and association. These movements became the precursors of current movements to challenge undemocratic practices of governments and to defend and protect human rights.

Moreover, when they confronted repressive governments, seeking to defend individual children and relatives, they were subjected to harassment, persecution and violence. Many became victimized by private and public security forces—suffering torture and rape. Ultimately, seeking justice for their family members, the mothers and women relatives of the disappeared confronted their situation as women—political rape created an understanding of gender abuse and gender inequality in power relations.

In the end, the movement of Mothers of the Disappeared opened an alternative space for political participation that mobilized people in forms other than those established by traditional political systems. The issue is no longer whether the movement is feminist or not feminist, but that it changed the lives of women and the way in which gender is perceived in traditional politics, leading to a questioning of power relations as they move from the individual, personal, and familial to the broader society.

Historically then, it becomes clear that for many Latin American women, the struggle to assert their rights and dignity as women is an integral part of the liberation movement of all peoples. We cannot liberate people without liberating women, and we cannot liberate women until we liberate all people.

Alicia, one of El Salvador's COMADRES, underscored this when she commented, "In the beginning of our struggle, it was an individual problem. But once we began to discover that there were others in the same situation, we realized we couldn't be isolated; that our struggle was collective." In other words, as Latinas, our struggle for equal rights is a struggle to create equality for women and men; to walk together on equal terms, and to create the conditions for the development of our collective potential as human beings.

This collective agenda is perhaps best expressed by the women of Chiapas who, at the invitation of the Zapatista Army of National

Liberation, attended a round of dialogues on indigenous affairs in November 1995. In a joint document, the women stated:

"We firmly state to all, that in our analysis of indigenous women, we conclude that the struggle is not against our men, but against a political and social and economic system, unjust and vertical, that permeates the attitudes of those who govern and are governed, and that break the equilibrium of social relations.

"We recognize that we are the basis of our culture and the givers of life, and that this role is given little value. Marginalization and poverty have been with us native people for over 503 years, and especially with women. We native people have long lived a history of colonialism and dependence that today is reproduced and heightened by the politics of neo-liberalism, the one-party system, the external debt, and a free trade agreement negotiated behind our backs and in conditions that disintegrate the national sovereignty. Pillage and the sale of our wealth by small groups that decided for all of us, men and women, in a society divided by classes, for a patriarchal and sexist ideology, that create unequal relations between men and women—these are also the characteristics of the current system.

"We women have decided to raise our voices to rescue our dignity and defend our rights. It is our view that our conditions as indigenous women will not improve if there is no improvement in the situation of the nation as a whole, our peoples, our communities."

In their statement, the women of Chiapas describe the essence of the Latina's struggle throughout history to the present day. It is this contradiction which the words of the women of Chiapas so eloquently address. The Zapatista women are also important because they articulate their positions both as women, and as members of the community and the nation.

Women in non-traditional politics like these confront head-on the issues of gender, class, and racial inequality. A *campesina* (a peasant woman) in Brazil said: "Yes, we women have been born with politics (in other words, integral to our being). When we are born, immediately we shout, we demand things, don't we? For this reason, we women have been born with politics."

As mentioned earlier, women as mothers are empowered to assert their moral authority in changing the nation and reclaiming what is crucial: human rights and dignity, including the right to participate in the decisions that affect their lives. By raising their voices before the political systems in power, these groups of women both in Latin America and the United States, challenge regimes and systems by taking the private domain—the family—and raising it to the level of public discourse.

Many women within these movements have become, and continue to be, victims of the particular social system they seek to change. In seeking justice for family members, women who have challenged state repression and violence have themselves endured personal suffering. Ultimately, movements such as the Mothers of the Disappeared open up an alternative forum for political participation that mobilizes people, which is perhaps the important aspect from a feminist viewpoint. This not only changes the lives of women, but also changes the way in which gender is perceived, which leads to a questioning of power relationships on both an individual and social level.

Women's political mobility and activism bring yet another challenge: as more women become activist, the violence against women increases, in both the family and society. According to a recent report of Amnesty International, violence against women in Mexico has increased, with an escalating pattern of torture, sexual abuse, political assassinations, and disappearances. Of the thirty-three cases of violence against Mexican women documented by Amnesty International, twenty-eight were victims of abuse for being activists in an opposition or civic group.

We cannot discuss violence against women without acknowledging the use of rape as state-imposed violence generated by conditions of war. Chiapas presents a vivid example. Under an ongoing siege described as low-intensity warfare, 60% of the Mexican Army surrounds the state. It is supported and financed by the United States Government. The use of rape in Chiapas is a deliberate strategy of war: over fifty-five rape cases against women have been documented. In a particular town in Chiapas recently, the private army, or White Guards, entered, and after setting aside the men, raped all the women in the village.

Our women's bodies have become the battlefield of this new type of genocide. Enclosed by the army, community life in Chiapas has been interrupted; hunger and disease prevail. As an invisible tactic, the slow death of the civilian population simultaneously and deliberately drives down civilian resistance and support for the Zapatistas. Ironically, it is the concentration of indigenous women in this struggle for justice that gives us lessons in dignity and commitment for family and nation.

In a letter which appeared in the Mexican newspaper *La Jornada* on January 26, 1994, Subcomandante Marcos of the *"Ejercito Zapatista de Liberación Nacional"* (Zapatista Army of National Liberation) related how the real uprising began: how in the process of consulting with the communities, which is the practice of the Zapatistas, many members traveled to surrounding communities to consider the various laws to be proposed in this revolutionary struggle. Susana, a member of the *"Comité Clandestino Revolucionario Indígena"* (Clandestine Revolutionary Indigenous Committee), which is the highest level of decision-making within the Zapatista army, consulted with the women in different communities to listen to their proposals. When the CCRI met again, the women were very clear about what they wanted: "We don't want to be forced to marry someone we do not want to marry. We want to have the number of children we want and can care for. We want the right to have leadership positions in the community. We want the right to have our say, and that it be respected. We want the right to study, and even to become drivers."

As similar petitions were heard from other women of the indigenous communities, the men from the CCRI grew silent. When the discourse ended, there was a long silence, after which one indigenous man said: "Well, I'm glad that my wife, my woman, doesn't know Spanish." A *"comandante,"* an indigenous woman, looked at him and responded, *"vete a la chingada!"* (screw you). We are going to translate the Women's Petition into all languages."

Marcos, in the same letter, reiterates the significance of the women's uprising in Chiapas: "But it is true," writes Marcos, "that the first rising of the EZLN was not January 1, 1994, but in March 1993, and this revolution was led by the Zapatista women."

I agree with the Zapatista women, the women from Chiapas, in their analysis, that in the world today all women face a particularly difficult challenge. The restructuring of economies and integration of economic blocks, as we know, is the work of transnational corporations. These corporations have skewed power structures and have redefined patterns of employment and degraded the quality of life throughout the world. What the Zapatistas call neo-liberalism— the impact of the global economy—is the challenge women face worldwide. It is against this siege of corporate globalization that women must now unite, not only to create life, but to create the conditions that sustain life and help it grow.

In this specific struggle, women are committed to building communities that will sustain a quality of life and maintain the dignity of all peoples within that community. This task is not our choice, but has been thrust upon us by the conditions generated by global integration and restructuring. The greatest challenge to the needs of the family is shaped by trends affecting the everyday lives of women resulting from globalization, economic restructuring and economic integration.

Worldwide women constitute 50% of the world's population yet own 1% of the world's property. One out of five families is headed by a single parent; 80% of these are women. The poverty rate of women heads-of-households is six times that of men heads-of-households. Women and their children work from 60 to 80 hours between job and household chores and tasks. Women earn 62 cents to a man's dollar; black women, 56 cents; Latinas 53 cents, Asian women 44, and disabled women, 24 cents.

An important trend in this globalization and economic restructuring is the gender subordination visible in the outcomes; both rely on and exacerbate the exploitation of women's time, energy, labor and sexuality. Women workers dominate some employment sectors which are seeing dramatic business restructuring: clerical, retail, finance, communications and light manufacturing. Corporate measures to reduce production costs, notably by cutting labor costs, have led to labor displacements, diminished the bargaining power of unions, increased risks to workers' health and safety and, in many instances, translate to downward economic slides for workers and their families.

Women are a growing and significant part of the labor force as work outside the home helps to sustain their families basic standard of living. Further still, many women already working outside the home have taken on a second job as a solution to a decline in family income. In the United States, three quarters of women between the 24 and 50 years of age are in the labor force and an estimated 3.3 million have more than one income-producing job. There is gender bias in corporate strategies to change employment patterns. A primary one is the increased use of part-time, seasonal, temporary or contract work. The majority affected are female and in certain industries are racial-ethnic minorities. Paid on an hourly basis, this female work force lacks benefits and union protection. One special part of this contingent work is done at home and therefore hidden, unregulated, unprotected and underpaid. In addition, women are represented disproportionately in the public service labor force where cuts are being made and privatization moves are occurring.

The consequences of these changes are enormous for women who make up a large proportion of the long-term unemployed, poorly qualified members of the work force in their roles as single parents, part-time workers in unskilled jobs, elderly workers, refugees and spouses of immigrant workers. According to the Bureau of the Census, the reality for women in the United States is as follows:

* Two-thirds of the official poor adults are female.
* The poverty rate for women of color is higher than for whites: African-American women have a 32 % poverty rate; Hispanic women, 29% and white women, 12%.
* 40% of official poor are children; it is especially acute for children of color, 46% for black, 41% for Hispanic children and 18% for white.
* The number of households headed by women has more than doubled since 1970. By 1992, women maintained 12 million families on their own.

Even where women and men share family responsibility, their lives are impacted by the restructuring of employment patterns which results in making temporary service jobs abundant, while services are being privatized. Men and women lose jobs and benefits. The burden of sustaining the family, of lessening tensions, of attempting to sustain adequate living conditions for all members of the family, becomes the burden of women. Women are the primary caregivers in families and caretakers of communities: the task is not only to birth new life but to take primary responsibility for nurturing families and communities so that life may flourish; to build social relationships so communities will cohere; and to raise future human beings so the world can prosper for the benefit of all its inhabitants.

As the global economy integrates and communities disintegrate, under the pressures of unemployment and under-employment, diminished social services, increased costs of private service, lack of adequate housing and growing violence in community and family, women are called on to sustain communities in stress. In response to these crises, women have developed and maintained social safety nets, such as domestic violence centers, shelters for runaway youth, soup kitchens for young and old, and youth oriented facilities. Women's time and energy are exploited as they become buffers to sustain families and communities in the midst of current policies of economic restructuring, integration and globalization.

This is precisely the challenge that the Zapatista women took on, and thus provide us with the most striking example of women whose lives have been impacted dramatically by these global changes. The communities where globalization has flourished were communities in which the global managers, despite the wealth of natural resources, had decided that the populations were expendable. The global managers themselves noted that at the time of the uprising, 50,000 people in Chiapas died of preventable diseases. A third of the children had received education, and very few of the women could read.

I recall once again the women of the Zapatista Army. When we traveled to Chiapas in August 1994 as part of the delegation of the National Commission, what impressed me most was the composition of the army itself. At least 35 to 40 % of the rank and file soldiers of the Zapatista Army were young, indigenous women. We had heard about Commanders Ramona, Anna María, Irma,

Elisa, and many others mentioned in the press. It was surprising, however, to see so many tiny young women of Mayan descent dressed in their uniforms, each carrying an M-16 covering half her body.

It saddened me that women, the givers of life, had to take up arms and be prepared to kill. I wondered about this decision that these young women had faced, and the conditions that drove them to kill, in order to give life to future generations. Perhaps the best answer to my question is the following letter from Subcomandante Marcos to the U.S. Representative of the Zapatistas, Cecilia Rodríguez, who in October 1995, was raped in Chiapas:

"The indigenous Zapatista women, who do not belong to us, but march at our side, those women, so far from the Conference of Beijing, those women, in a struggle against everything and against everyone (and this includes us, the Zapatista men), those Zapatista women have decided to stop being women in order to have the right to be a woman."

These are women who decided to stop reproducing generations that would live in poverty and humiliation, women who decided to change the traditional cultural definition of how they would be defined as women, women who ultimately will join the many who made a decision to die to give life, and yet these masked, faceless women facing death in the highlands of Chiapas, took time on March 8 of this year, to pay tribute to all of us, to all the women with dignity, the ones who struggle.

And I would like to close with those words from a communiqué, from these women to us, on March 8, International Women's Day:

"Today we want to salute our sisters who have fallen in the two years of the military encirclement, to our dead.

"Today we want to salute also all the women who have helped us so that our voice is heard.

"Today we want to salute all of the women who have seen in the Zapatistas, a mirror of their own dignity and rebellion.

"Today we want to salute all the women who struggle everywhere, so that nowhere is being a woman a shame, a nightmare, an adornment.

"Today, we want to salute all women who have dignity and who struggle.

"Salud, women in struggle.

Health, women with dignity. "

Photo © Danna Byrom, 1996.

Pat Cuney

Foundation for a Compassionate Society
Stonehaven Goddess Program

As I move into the more formal parts of this presentation, I also want to stop and thank Genevieve Vaughan for her commitment to women and feminist values and to global and local feminist activism. We've said it a number of times tonight, and I don't think it can be said too often, this entire conference is her gift to international feminism.

Like the other women who work at the Foundation, I consider it an honor and a privilege to work for an organization that was founded to demonstrate women's values in the context of modeling the gift economy, of which Genevieve Vaughan is a primary theoretician.

The woman I am introducing tonight can stand on her record any time, anywhere. We honor her both for who she is and what she has done. She travels in this and other countries as a lecturer and feminist organizer, and is a frequent spokesperson on issues of equality. Currently she is a writer and consulting editor for Ms. Magazine, the international feminist bi-monthly that she co-founded in 1972, a periodical that changed a generation.

Among her books are *"Moving Beyond Words," "Revolution from Within: a Book of Self-Esteem;" "Outrageous Acts and Everyday Rebellions," and "Marilyn/Norma Jeane,"* about Marilyn Monroe.

She helped found the Women's Action Alliance, a national center for information and advocacy in such areas as non-sexist, multi-racial children's education, and communication among women's groups; the National Women's Political Caucus, and the Coalition of Labor Union Women.

She is president of Voters for Choice and the founding president of the Ms. Foundation for Women, which is a national multi-racial women's fund that supports grass-roots projects to empower women

Photo © Danna Byrom, 1996.

and girls. She has raised funds for many campaigns, especially those of women and candidates of color. She worked for Caésar Chávez, the United Farm Workers, and other civil rights groups.

In 1993 she was inducted in the National Women's Hall of Fame in Seneca Falls, New York. While history may record her most significant achievement as the founder of Ms. Magazine, for myself, I am especially grateful for her consistent willingness to cross race and class barriers, something the women's movements of the 1800's and 1920's were never able to successfully address, something we are struggling with today.

And I am also grateful to her for her willingness in her books and in her articles to share with us the truth about her own life, because when one woman tells the truth about her life, the rest of us realize that we are not alone.

For me, it is a lifetime achievement just to have the honor of introducing her to you. Let us welcome GLORIA STEINEM.

Photo © Danna Byrom, 1996.

Gloria Steinem

Writer, Consulting Editor, Ms. Magazine, Voters for Choice,
Women's Action Alliance

I've always wanted to live to be a hundred. Now I know why. I have to—in order to live up to this introduction. But when one woman shows emotion, then we also know that none of us is alone.

Photo © Danna Byrom, 1996.

Did you meet each other during the intermission? I hope you did, but if not, here is your assignment: Look around you before you leave the room or on your way out, see three or four people you don't know, introduce yourselves, say what you care about, what you're doing. If you've come here today, you probably share a lot of interests and values, so you can skip right past the first six weeks of lunches, and say what's in your heart. Then see if you don't leave here with a new friend, a new subversive organizing tactic, a new job, a new love affair—anything could happen! During the question and answer period, I also hope we can overturn the hierarchy of us up here as speakers and you down there, so we can have a powerful organizing meeting.

I would like to start by telling you about my trip last summer to the Kalahari desert with Rebecca Adamson, a Native American activist who is head of the First Nations Development Institute. She had been asked by the Kwei or San people of the Kalahari—indigenous people also known as the Bush People—to consult about land rights and economic development projects. She invited me and a few other activists to come along. So we flew to Johannesburg, then got another plane to a small town in Botswana, and then another little plane, and then rode hours in a Land Rover—until we were in the middle of the Kalahari Desert.

And there we were, literally thousands of miles from the nearest settlement, under an enormous sky, with a group of about twelve Bush people, women, men and children. Over those few days, I learned a little bit, just a little bit, about the subtlety, concerns, and sophistication of this indigenous group that is such a resource of great wisdom and knowledge for all of us—as indeed all the indigenous groups on every continent are. Yet the Bush People are thought by many in Botswana itself to be underdeveloped, unsophisticated, undesirable. They aren't even allowed a designation as a tribal group. Until the 1960s, there were hunting licenses—we were told it was legal, you could get a license to kill a Bush person.

These gentle people showed us a little of their way of life. The women took us out into what appeared to be empty desert with straggly bushes dotting the sands, and they showed us how they dig with their digging sticks for roots that are excellent to eat. They also showed us the root that is used for migraine headaches, another root for contraception, and another root that women use to render themselves sterile when they decide they have enough children. In general, a woman has two or three children spaced several years apart.

They showed us their games, very joyous games, the goals of which were not competition, but cooperation. They did a trance dance for us, which lasted most of the night, and was about spirituality, and also healing. They explained to us that both men and women are responsible for children, and I believed them, because the only child who cried was one whose father had been forced off the land in order to get a job. The little boy missed his father, just as he would his mother.

For Bush People, there are some sex-differentiated roles, but in general both men and women hunt—though the men hunt for large animals, and the women catch smaller animals, as well as gather food. There is no value put on virginity. In girls or in boys, children are encouraged to play together, sexually or otherwise.

When they are old enough to be self-sufficient, children build their own huts and live together. It's all right to have sex between boys and girls, between girls and girls, or between boys and boys, as part of experimentation, part of learning what grown-up life is like. Children become sexual in the same integrated way that they learn about hunting, weaving, trance-dances, stories and all the enormously sophisticated cultural knowledge that is their way of life.

I tell you this partly because I can't *not* tell you. Because these are an endangered people. They are being persecuted and pushed off their land. The last three thousand people living in the Kalahari are being pushed out of their way of life, and with them goes an immense source of human knowledge about how to live in balance with each other and nature, a kind of human rain forest of wisdom. I also tell you this because it is hard for us to imagine different family forms, different kinds of values, unless we know they existed somewhere. But, in fact, each of us, no matter what continent or culture we come from, can find a basis for alternative family values in what is so suspiciously called "pre-history"—which just means pre-patriarchy, pre-racism, pre-nationalism. That's why they don't teach us about it, right? Yet these ancient ways are part of our heritage. I think it's comforting to know that life in various forms and with certain shared values—a connection to nature, a sense of balance, a lack of ownership and cooperative forms of human organization—this "alternative" way of life went on for 95% of human history. The last eight to ten thousand years about which our patriarchal culture teaches us—and it's usually much less than that—is less than 5% of human history.

So I suggest that we just declare the last five-to-ten thousand years an experiment that failed. Let's declare this the first meeting of the post-patriarchal, post-racist, post-nationalist age. I think Native American poet and novelist Paula Gunn Allen is right when she says, in *"The Sacred Hoop,"* that "the root of oppression is the loss of memory."

I also agree with Cherokee scholar and writer Rayna Green, who says that true feminism—women's liberation, womanism, self-government, autonomy, self-authority, self-determination, whatever we want to call it—is really memory on this continent. Because many of our ideas about individual human dignity and democracy within families—about non-hierarchical forms of organization and balance with nature—came from cultures that were already on this continent millennia before Europeans arrived. That's where they were learned, not from some idea of democracy in Greece that actually had a very limited idea of democracy and kept slaves. Yet Native groups have been so de-humanized by history in order to justify their persecution and genocide that we ourselves don't understand how much our ancestors learned from them.

We must remember that what now is called "Women's History," "Native American History," "African American History," or "Asian American History" really ought to be called "Remedial History." I don't know about you, but I didn't learn about the female plus people-of-color part of history when I was going to school. So I am continually amazed and angered when I learn that, for example, the entire state of Florida was governed by a coalition of Seminole Indians and freed or runaway slaves. For many years, they fought off the entire U.S. government. Or when I learn that Mozart had an older sister, Nannerl, whom he considered "the really talented one." She was sent home to marry, but some musicologists think compositions attributed to him might really be hers.

Somebody gave me a button once that said, "The truth will make you free, but first it will piss you off."

I also didn't learn in school that our form of government and constitution were inspired in part by the Iroquois Confederacy. Of course, our forefathers still didn't get it right; they left out women, who declared war and peace, and chose the male chief in the Iroquois Nations. I didn't know until a few years ago that the women of the abolitionist and suffragist movements—like Sojourner Truth, Matilda Gage, Elizabeth Cady Stanton and others—knew, visited with, learned from, and wrote about women in those Native American cultures, and held such cultures up as examples of the kind of society they were striving to create.

In a way, early American feminists were talking about feminism as theory. But indigenous women were often living it as practice. Moreover, when Engels wrote his essay on "The Origin of the Family, Private Property and the State," he based much of it on the work of anthropologist Lewis Henry Morgan and his published studies of the Iroquois Confederacy.

So indigenous cultures were and are among the roots of feminism, socialism, the idea of communalism, communal ownership, a different relationship with nature, and so on. They still exist in some form on every continent—embattled, almost annihilated, subject to genocide. But they still exist.

I think that gives us some hope. It isn't that we can go back to the past. We can't. Nor should we romanticize the past. But we need to know that changes we're now told are impossible—living with feminist values, changed forms of organization, our insistence that violence is never an acceptable way of solving conflict but only for self-defense—all these have existed in some form. When they tell us, "You can't change that; it's human nature," we need to have the knowledge that for 95% of human time on earth, there existed a very different vision of human nature.

I think the first thing we need to re-consider about "family values" is saying "family" in the singular. That is a right wing trip altogether. The minute you say "family" in the singular, it defines one kind of family as normal and renders all other forms peripheral or wrong. The truth is there have always been many, many different kinds of families—extended families, communal families, families in which, in the African tradition, children were raised by the grandparents, because it was thought that someone young enough to have a child was not wise enough to raise it.

There have always been committed, nurturing relationships between men, between women and also chosen relationships, adopted relationships. Certainly, native cultures on this continent often adopted people who were of different nations, different races into their extended families. The patriarchal, nuclear family that we are supposed to think is the normal and only one, that kind of family is really only about one-hundred-and-fifty-years-old, and is almost entirely the function of industrialization and capitalism. It was a form invented to make people portable, so they could be shipped about at the will of their employers, something that could not be done with big, extended, communal families.

Even in recent agricultural communities, women in patriarchal families still played important economic roles. It was industrialization that took fathers out of the home and made them the only wage earners for the first time—causing women and children to be entirely dependent on men.

The idea that there is only one family form is really pure bullshit. Nonetheless, we have to get a grip on what the right wing means when it says "family values," because otherwise, we will be in a continual state of shock and surprise. It may seem illogical to us; it is not illogical. It has logic of its own. As family, they are talking about the male-headed, patriarchal nuclear household. That is precisely what they mean and that is all they mean. That is why they call "anti-family" any guarantee of rights for women or children, because such rights interfere with the patriarchal authority of the male head of household.

So to them, the Equal Rights Amendment was "anti-family," because it was a guarantee of rights to women. Laws against child abuse are also "anti-family," which is why they are trying to de-fund such programs. Battered women's shelters—which they call "runaway wives" shelters—are absolutely "anti-family." Once you get a grip on what they mean by "family," they are actually logical.

For instance, their "family values" say that abortion is murder, but capital punishment and war are fine. This at first would seem rather odd, but their point is not what is done, but who does it. So long as the state or the church or the corporation or the multi-national does it, it's okay. But if the individual does it, if we have the power, it's subversion and it's not okay. The state can take any number of lives through capital punishment, and multi-nationals can pollute and destroy in the name of profit. But a woman can't decide whether or not to bear a child.

Among their values is the idea—and this seems like another sort of illogic—that both birth control and lesbianism are wrong. You have to get a grip on what they mean. What they mean is that women's bodies—which are the most basic means of production, the means of reproduction—have to be under patriarchal control, and dedicated to having children, who are then patriarchally owned. Therefore, any form of sexual expression that doesn't end in conception inside patriarchal marriage—so that the children arc properly owned—is wrong. Therefore, both lesbianism and birth control are wrong. They are not illogical. But I think there is something else here that is deeper than logic. What we are talking about is *content*; what they are talking about is *form*. They are talking about *who has the power to do something*; we are talking about *what that something is*. We are trying to give each other the power to control our own lives. They are trying to control the lives of others. We say the power to make our own decision matters more than the decisions we choose to make. They say that disobedient decisions are wrong *per se*.

We are really redefining power. We no longer mean that power is the ability to make other people do something. We mean that power is the ability to control our own destiny, to control our own lives, and to be in a community of others with equal power.

If we do away with "family" in the singular and say "families," if we de-emphasize *form* and emphasize *content*, we will go a long way towards creating and living feminist family values.

There is, however, an insight we share with the ultra right wing. As feminists, women's liberationists, whatever it is we wish to call ourselves—we understand something liberals often miss: *There is a direct line between the kind of families we have and the kind of society we create.* If you look at democracies, you will find that they have all rested on some degree of democracy in the household, in the way people were raised. If you look at authoritarian and totalitarian states, you will find that they all spring from the training ground of the hierarchical, dictatorial family.

But in the same way that no one studies the 95 % of human history that preceded patriarchal hierarchy, families and households as the training ground of democracy are a vast unstudied part of human experience—and certainly a subject unstudied by political scientists.

If you read the papers, for example, you might think that the sole reason that democracy has emerged in Eastern Europe and the former Soviet Union had to do with economic deterioration under communist rule. Actually, economic conditions in the past 25 years were better than they had been in previous years. Or you might assume that our arms build-up had something to do with what was happening, that the Soviet Union responded to Ronald Reagan and his right wing friends marching around calling it "evil" and "godless."

Of course, there are always many factors at work, but one important and usually ignored factor is the relationship between the way children are raised and the political forms that result. Before the Russian Revolution, religious fervor combined with feudal society to create forms of child rearing that were quite authoritarian and abusive. For one thing, religion suppressed contraception, and people had too many children. Because they couldn't care for all these babies while they went out to the fields, they often left children swaddled—tied to boards with rags—and left immobilized in these urine-soaked rages for the entire day. Children were also beaten as discipline, an abuse justified by a religious theory of child-rearing—one we recognize in this country, too—which treated children as little animals whose spirits had to be broken.

Can you imagine any better way to induce cultural passivity than being tied to a board as an infant? Can you imagine any deeper way of learning that nothing you do matters? Can you imagine any training in violence more effective than imbedding it in your earliest relationship to the world?

As you know, when bad things happen to kids, they come to think they are bad people. They grow up believing they need authoritarian leaders to discipline them, that whatever goes wrong is their fault and that their only hope of change is to grow up and impose their will on others.

If you look at the background of despots in all parts of the world, you will find that they themselves were often sadistically abused kids. They grew up believing there were only two choices: either be the victim or the victimizer. For instance, Stalin was a sadistically abused kid. I am not a childhood determinist, mind you. I believe violent childhoods can be healed, and patterns can change, but when they do not change, the violence keeps being acted out. It has the deep power of feeling like home.

In the Soviet Union, patterns gradually changed after the revolution. As society became more secular and the birthrate went down, children were raised with a little more humanity and individual attention, so you got people like Gorbachev, who was a gently-bred child. Because his will and self-authority were more respected by his elders, he could imagine that other people could also make decisions for themselves. Thus, a Russian leader emerged who could begin to imagine the possibility of self-government and democracy. So did a large number of people who could make their own decisions instead of being passive.

The good—the bad—people experience in families is writ large in the world of politics, culture and foreign policy. For instance, there are studies of good Samaritans during World War II, people who helped Jews even though they themselves were not Jewish, and even though they were risking their own lives. I find it fascinating that their single, most often shared characteristic seems to be that they were not severely abused as children. Without abuse, there is no fear and trauma to cut off the natural leap of empathy for other human beings. If you see someone else in trouble, you empathize instead of trying to disassociate. But abuse, violence, neglect, ridicule, humiliation, sexual abuse—all these things interrupt the natural flow of empathy. They close us down emotionally. They make us feel that we must either conquer or be conquered.

So nothing, nothing, *nothing* could be more important than the kinds of families we create, whether they are chosen families, biological families, extended families, whatever forms they take, nothing could be more important than the content of respect, democracy, nurturing and compassion, because it will be writ large in the world.

Personally I agree with Mililani about gender, because it is culturally created. Gender roles are not the same from one culture to the next. They are not about biology; they are about culture. Hopefully, one day there will be no gender; there will be humanity instead. Because the truth is that each of us contains the full circle of human qualities. Each is also a unique miracle that could never have happened before and could never happen again, because our unique blend of millennia of particular heredity and particular environment could never happen again. In male-dominant cultures, however, 75% of human qualities are arbitrarily called "masculine," leaving about 25% which are called "feminine." If you list them and ask people which qualities are masculine and which are feminine, that's the way it turns out. So naturally, women are on the forefront of revolution, because we have more to gain. We've lost 75% of ourselves. But men have a lot to gain, too. They've lost 25% of themselves.

We're all trying to become whole people. I think the chance to develop the full circle of human qualities is always with us, but it's easier the younger we are, and the less damaged we are. Even in concept, however, I think we're only half-way there—even in our imaginations.

We have imagined that women can do what men can do, and so we've convinced most of the country. But most of us haven't convinced ourselves that men can do what women can do, and so we haven't convinced the country. Many of us have had the courage to raise our daughters more like our sons, which is great, because they are more whole people. But few of us have had the courage to raise our sons more like our daughters—and so there are fewer men raising children than there are women achieving outside the home.

Until, as in Kwei culture, boys are raised to raise children, until men raise and nurture babies and little children as much as women do, both males and females are going to be cursed with the prison of gender. Kids are going to grow up thinking that, if they are boys, they can't be loving and nurturing. Girls are going to grow up thinking they must be loving and nurturing and can't be daring in the world outside the home, just because they are girls. Masculinity will continue to be culturally emphasized in unbalanced ways. Gender status will have to be earned through violent or controlling behavior to be "a man," and through passive and submissive behavior to be "a woman." And this will continue to be the deepest model for racial roles and class roles.

Often, we are overwhelmed by the enormity of the work there is to do. After all, we have to overthrow or humanize—you can pick your verb depending on how patient you feel today—patriarchy, racism, nationalism, multi-national corporations, hierarchy itself; just a few little things like that. That's why I think it's helpful to think about who lived on this land 20,000 years ago, 50,000 years ago.

We also need to look at our own personal history and see how far we have come. And we have to realize that, in fact, everything we do matters. The art of behaving morally, ethically, is behaving as if everything we do matters—because it does. Marx got a lot of things right, but one thing he didn't get right was his idea that the end justifies the means. In fact, the means *is* the end. The means we choose dictate the ends we achieve. We must always remember that as we pursue feminist family values.

If we feel discouraged, we can take heart in the new physics, which tells us that the world itself is not hierarchical, but a kind of orderly chaos in which everything is both independent—and interdependent. We can remember that the flap of a butterfly's wings here can change the weather hundreds of miles away.

Everything we do matters. Everything we do has enormous power. We are a continuum of the past. Together, all of us in this room—and the world could be a lot more like this room—make one hell of a butterfly.

Photo © Danna Byrom, 1996.

María Limón

Poet and Writer
Foundation for a Compassionate Society

My name is María Limón, and I'd like to thank everyone who came from so far away and welcome them to Occupied Mexico. Some of us still remember!

I've been hard-pressed to introduce a woman who needs no introduction, a woman who is history. So I've been walking around for the last few days asking people what they think of when they her the name Angela Davis.

Ana Sisnett spoke of possibilities and presence. The simple knowledge that Angela was a professor of philosophy at UCLA opened the possibilities of being in ways that Ana had never seen before.

Lillian Stevens thinks of traffic tickets. She spoke of how her introduction to the revolution was to have her driver's license revoked because of all the traffic tickets she got when she refused to remove her 'Free Angela Davis and All Political Prisoners' bumper sticker from her car. Police, she said, would drop out of the sky to give her tickets.

Erin Rogers spoke of how Angela's last presentation at UT changed not only her life but the entire political context on campus. Erin said the presentation helped get Toni Luckett, a black lesbian,

Photo © Danna Byrom, 1996.

elected as student body president.

And for this *chicanita* from *Aztlán*, Angela Davis represents vast and open possibilities.

Angela Davis is a woman who maintains the integrity required of anyone who holds their commitment to struggle against all forms of oppression. And this Ms. Davis has done for decades throughout this country's contemporary political history, at great personal risk. My life has been changed by her words, challenged by her example, and enriched by her presence on this planet.

Today Angela Davis is a tenured professor in the History of Consciousness program at U.C. Santa Cruz. She received the distinguished honor of an appointment to the University of California Presidential Chair in African American and Feminist Studies.

As Patti Salas put it, Angela Davis is the most *chingona* professor on the planet. Roughly translated, it means that she's one powerful woman. She talks the talk and walks the walk in some of the most difficult places among the most challenging situations.

Ms. Davis continues her work advocating for prisoner's rights. She conducted a series of interviews with incarcerated women for a research project that seeks to develop ideas for new progressive legislation around the penal system.

And Angela Davis the writer and thinker continues to provoke, inspire, and urge others to keep thinking and working right alongside her with essays, articles, and a forthcoming book with the working title of "*Gertrude 'Ma' Rainey, Bessie Smith, and Billie Holiday: Black Women's Music and Social Consciousness.*"

Please help me welcome professor Angela Davis.

Angela Davis

Activist, Professor, History of Consciousness Department
University of California, Santa Cruz

It is an honor to be able to address you after having listened to the wonderful, inspiring words of Mililani Trask and María Jiménez and Gloria Steinem. I was sitting there, thinking to myself—what is there left to say?

I want to begin by suggesting that particularly at this time in the history of our country and the history of the globe, radical activism is needed more than ever before. I also want to suggest that women and women's issues need to be at the forefront in this radical activism. Some of you might think it's archaic to talk about radical activism. After all, activism is generally associated with a generation that is approximately the age of your parents.

Something else began to bother me somewhat as I listened to

these powerful words. I asked myself—who is the youngest among us? I think our panel should have included a few women who are much younger. One of the issues that we really need to address is intergenerational communication and particularly the importance of accepting young women as leaders. As a matter of fact, I don't think we can move forward if young women and young people are not at the forefront of our struggles. You have to be a little young and crazy to get out there and do the things that are necessary in order to try to change the world.

Consider that everyone sitting on the stage this evening became involved in social movements at a very young age. So where are you who are presently the age we were at the beginning of our social involvements? The next time there's an enormous gathering like this, some of you will need to be up here as well.

There are so many challenges facing us, challenges which require us to think in feminist, anti-racist, anti-homophobic, anti-capitalist ways. As a matter of fact, this evening's theme revolves around new values, feminist values. Those values have to be anti-racist and anti-capitalist values. And the challenge of the women's movement today is to figure out how to turn back this terrible tide of reaction that threatens to overcome all of us. These are dangerous times, very dangerous times.

How can we prevent the attempt to dismantle affirmative action programs all over the country for people of color and for women of all racial and ethnic backgrounds. What can we do to stop the rise of immigrant bashing?

I come here from California, I'm sad to say. California is the state where immigrants from Mexico—people from Central America who are called immigrants—are under attack. However, I don't think there is anyone in this country who has the right not to call herself or himself an immigrant, except indigenous people. In California, people from Mexico and Central America are cruelly beaten by the police, such as in the Riverside incident. California has passed Proposition 187, which denies education and health care to undocumented immigrants.

How can we prevent the criminalization and demonization of people who are called non-citizens? How can we prevent the incarceration of ever-increasing numbers of men and of women as well? The rate of increase in the arrest of women is about twice that of the rate of increase in the arrest and incarceration of men. So if you look at the historical trajectory down the line, across the millennium, vast numbers of women—most of them will be women of color—will populate the jails and prisons. We will be facing an exploding punishment industry that will claim large numbers of women as its victims.

How can we prevent the overruling of the educational system by the prison system? How can we bring an end to sexual violence, and how can we integrate a challenge to homophobia into all of the work that we do? I have just listed some of the urgent questions facing us. This is the most complicated historical moment we have ever experienced.

Young, emerging activists, tend to romanticize the 60s. We must totally dismiss the notion that radicalism is a uniquely 60s phenomena. Oftentimes people who moved into social-political activism during the 60s tend to respond nostalgically to the challenges that I've listed, and tend to assume that, "Well, if only we could organize now like we organized back then things would be different."

But during that period, when the student movement swept the country, when the civil rights movement and movements in Latino, Black, Asian American, Native American communities began to develop and become widespread, when the Women's Movement emerged, our notions of struggle were rather simple. We embraced a rather simplistic notion of who counted as the enemy and who counted as a friend. As a matter of fact, we could draw a line and argue that everyone on the other side of the line was the enemy. Sometimes that line was a racial line, sometimes that line was a gender line, sometimes that line was a class line, but we knew who the enemy was! No doubt about it!

In those days, what we have come to call "interlocking oppressions" or a "matrix of domination" or "intersecting oppressions" were unheard of. This notion of a complicated interaction of categories of gender and class and sexuality and race mutually determining one another, had not even been conceptualized. As a matter of fact, if you think back to the Civil Rights period, gender, as we know it, hadn't been seriously considered. Gloria was talking about the ultimate withering away of gender, but during the Civil Rights period we didn't even have the word "gender," within our political vocabularies.

As a matter of fact, as the Women's Movement emerged, we tended to use the word "sex." Sexuality wasn't in the picture; the word "homophobia" hadn't even been invented. But at the same time it is really important for us to understand today that those movements, however simplistic they may have been from the historical perspective of those of us who are situated in the late 1990s, changed many of our common sense notions. They changed the common sense of the entire country—our common sense notions of race, gender; of race and racism, of gender and misogyny.

Since the Reagan-Bush era, what we have witnessed is the rise of a conservative movement that has managed by now to reverse those common sense notions which we transformed through movement and struggle. They have been successful to the extent that today many people assume racism no longer exists. When something like the beating of a black man in Los Angeles takes place, it is interpreted as a horrible hold-over from an era that has long been transcended.

If you look at the assumption on which the arguments against affirmative action are made, it is that racism no longer exists because many of the laws, according to which discrimination was legally authorized, have been changed. However, today racism is more profoundly inscribed in the political economy of the United States than ever before. Racism is more strongly entangled with misogyny than ever before.

It's true that black people may not be told today where to sit on buses and trains or where to eat or where to go to school, or where to live, but racism is still very much at work in determining who goes to prison and who doesn't, who is destined to rely on the welfare system, and who isn't; who is considered an immigrant and scapegoated in multiple ways, and who isn't. One of the things we need to think very deeply about is the extent to which we tend to conceive of issues of race in black/white terms. We need to move beyond the black/white binary in the way we think about issues of race. That, of course, is especially important in this part of the country, where there are large numbers of Chicanos, Latinos and Native Americans.

Many people have pointed out that affirmative action isn't as new as it appears to be. It is assumed that it came about as a result of the Civil Rights struggle. Affirmative action models were developed as far back as the New Deal. As a matter of fact, Karen Brodkin Sachs has written an article which is entitled, "How Jews Became White Folks." She points out that the New Deal benefits (the GI Bill, for example,) created an economic base for Jews and ethnic Europeans. It wasn't so much by their own bootstraps that they pulled themselves up. They were helped by the government. And the fact is, large numbers of GIs of color received dishonorable discharges, and therefore were not eligible for the GI Bill. So that's something to think about as we debate the merits of affirmative action for people of color and women of all racial backgrounds.

I want to join with all my sisters who emphasize the importance of looking at our local struggles within a global context. It is essential to think about transnational capitalism these days—and to think deeply about the extent to which people equate "democratic values" with "capitalist values." This is a point that Chandra Mohanty has eloquently made.

It is feminists' responsibility to contest that equation, and to legitimize open critiques of capitalism. We can't be satisfied with this system. Many people assume that socialism didn't work. It didn't work in the Soviet Union and Eastern Europe, because of the lack of economic and political democracy. That might be true, but we need to emphasize that those specific socialist experiments didn't work. That does not mean that there is no possibility of envisioning a social system beyond capitalism. We cannot be content with this system.

And I think I have the right to say, at my age, (and I have entered my second half-century), that I have struggled too long and too hard to give up at this point. Let's just talk for a moment about the ways in which transnational capital migrates all over the world, at will. It does not recognize national borders, and often the very routes that are carved out by transnational corporations fleeing organized labor and seeking cheap labor pools, are the circuits that are used by people who then come from those countries to the United States.

But we don't hear criticisms of immigrant corporations, do we? These corporations are fleeing organized labor. At the present time only 12% of the labor force in this country is organized. That is even less than when the great organizing drives began in the 1930s. Communities literally die as a result of the fact that these corporations close down shop. They leave an economic vacuum; people lose their jobs, the tax base for education disappears, and then, of course, new economies move.

And what are those new economies? (Response from audience: "WalMart!") No. If people in a community don't have a job and therefore don't have money, WalMart is not going to move into that community because nobody will be able to shop there—not even at WalMart. These alternate economies are drug economies, economies in sexual services. And that, in turn, leads people directly into the punishment industry. These are the people who are then criminalized; these are the people who are identified as "the enemy."

At the same time, so-called anti-crime ideologies flourish. Evoke the notion of crime and people are willing to do anything, the most cruel things imaginable, like putting six-year old kids in Juvenile Hall. Granted, the six-year-old boy in the San Francisco Bay Area did a horrible thing when he beat up an infant. But since when do you put children that age in jail, or convict parents whose son committed a crime for not sufficiently supervising the son? You see where "family" values will take you; they will take you toward fascism.

The criminal is usually figured as a young black man. As a matter of fact, 32.5 % of all young black men between 20 and 29 are now in prison. In California, 40 % of all young black men are in prison. In California, 75 % of all young black men have been arrested at one time or another.

And of course, when you look at those people who are in prison, the majority are there for non-assaultive crimes. But when we think about convicts, who do we think about? Most often people associate criminals with child-molesters, murderers, ect. That is the basis on which fear is generated, which then makes it impossible for people to think critically about the punishment industry which is creating an increasingly incarcerated society.

Then we have the ideological figure of the immigrant which strikes fear into the hearts of many people in this country. This is a racism which is embraced by people of color as well in this anti-immigrant campaign.

I want to conclude by making some suggestions regarding organizing strategies. In order to meet the very complicated challenges we face as we move toward the next millennium, our consciousness needs to reflect the complexity of the way our lives are structured. Bernice Reagan has pointed out, and many of you have probably read her essay, that coalitional work needs to be a central strategy in late 20th century organizing practices.

We have to start thinking in political terms. We have to begin to politicize our identities; to consider our identities not fixed, but flexible identities, that can be established in accordance with the political projects we do and political goals that we posit. In the work that we are doing, we need to do unlikely coalitional work. We need to create formations that are based on the notion of unlikely coalitions.

What I've been thinking about are coalitions between students and prisoners, for example. Students and prisoners can work together, because that's the only way to save the educational system. Otherwise, the punishment industry is going to devour all of the funds that ought to be directed toward the educational system.

Another coalition that should be encouraged is one that would bring together the welfare rights activists and gay and lesbian activists, because both welfare mothers and gays and lesbians are directly targeted by the racialized and sexualized conservative emphasis on "family values." Maybe we need to have more marches. What would a march look like with welfare mothers and gays and lesbians? Not that the two are mutually exclusive, but that would be a very powerful demonstration.

We also need to think about coalitional work that brings together both documented and undocumented immigrants on the one hand, and young African American, Asian American, Latino, Native American youth who are all targeted by this devious criminalization process that replaces the legitimate need for jobs, education and health care with a very effective demonization of all these groups.

In this context it is certainly time to revise the demand for a reconsideration of the 8-hour day. We need a shorter work day. Gloria was talking about history and memory. The 8-hour day hasn't been around forever. Workers fought for an 8-hour day because they had a 10-hour day. Before that, they fought for the 10-hour day because they were working 12 hours a day. And certainly with this crisis that we're facing, one of the ways that we could envision jobs for undocumented immigrants, as well for vast numbers of unemployed youths in communities of color, would be a shorter work day.

These are a few of my own ideas. I know that there are young people in the audience who can come up with some ideas that are far more radical, and far more appealing, because you have a sense of what people, young women and men of your generation, are prepared to do.

I want to conclude by thanking the Foundation for Compassionate Society, Genevieve Vaughan, and all of the wonderful women whom you've seen and heard from today for giving us the opportunity to come together, to hold hands with each other, and to think creatively and radically about the possibilities of the future.

Thank you very much.

Photo © Danna Byrom, 1996.

Dialogue

Question: A lot of the laws that are placed on us aren't really created by us. A lot of them are patriarchal, made to keep us down, I'm wondering how you feel about activism that breaks the law.

Angela: Civil disobedience is great.

Question cont: So go out there, and if you don't agree with the law, do you let them know that?

Angela: Civil disobedience is a proven tactic of struggle. It has a long history, but it needs to be organized.

Question: I'm 27, I'm trying to go back and get my Master's Degree. I'm working, I'm making in the low twenties, and I want to know how everybody gets the energy and the time—with my over eight-hour-a-day job and I have no children—I still can't seem to find enough time. By the time I'm done, in bed, it's eleven or twelve at night, and I'm tired, and I haven't even done anything that you have done, I haven't even read the books that I want to read—

Gloria: I think that we need to think of social revolution as something that is just part of our lives. If we think it has to be a big thing, we put it off. Then we never do it. But if we just say to ourselves: I'm going to write five outrageous letters every week. I'm going to give 10% of my salary to social justice of some kind, whatever it is you think you want to give it to, I mean, it's the best investment you'll ever make. The money isn't going to be worth anything next year anyway. I'm going to go to one demonstration a month just to keep my blood tingling, whatever.

I think also that women are without a country or a neighborhood, so I find it very helpful to have a group of women I can meet with once a week and be encouraged by them. You can think of outrageous things to do together.

Question: How did you all know this was want you wanted to do?

Mililani: One of the things about human rights and social justice work is that it is exhausting, and burn-out is something that we all suffer from, and what we have to remember is that part of being a woman is sustaining yourself. One of the things that we have to guard against is our tendency to give so much that we bankrupt our own spirit.

Also you have to set priorities for yourself, and you have to remember, that spiritual balance is the wellspring of our energy. If you're to lead your nation, you have to have a spiritual balance. Sometimes, I have to withdraw from things, but the Creator, and the Spirit, is what renews us. It's the wellspring of our culture, so prayer is something that is not often spoken of at meetings like this, but is a way to find a connection to our women's spirit.

As to feeling the calling, you know, I fought against it for many years. I tried all kinds of things. I thought when I went to law school I was going to make money, have a Jaguar. But, it never did happen to me, and I found that there was a great calling that I had. If I had heard it when I was at your age, I probably, if I had heard and not denied it, I probably would have had a much happier life. But we have all these things that the paternalistic society puts on you, so you go into, "I can't be this or I can't be that."

The thing to do is to listen to your heart, and when you hear that call, if you know that it is for you, walk that path. If it doesn't fit you, discard it. A good test is when nighttime comes, if you cannot sleep with what you have done that day, with what you have said, you know you are doing the wrong thing. You are asking hard questions!

Question: I just wanted to say that I've never been to a place where you could really get up and talk about —I really had a good time . . .

Question: Recently there was something called the Million Man March. Whatever happened to the Million Women March? I'd like to throw that question open to the panel.

Angela: That's a hard question.

Question: Why don't you organize it, Angela?

Angela: I don't think we need to organize something in response to the Million Man March, because I think the politics of that march were deeply problematic, were very much formed by the kind of conservative family values that we're trying to contest here. So I think we need to do something new.

As a matter of fact, I want to ask you to figure out what that new thing is we should be doing.

Question: My experiences as an activist have always been coupled with a lot of disillusionment and self-sacrifice and pain. I'm not as active now as I should be, and your challenge brings a lot to the fore. I wonder how, I mean, I am young, and I'm thinking about the future—

Angela: How old are you?

Question: Twenty-three. If I do this —

Angela: You already have your activist era behind you?

Question: And I'm already taking a break. That's what worries me.

Angela: Have you ever had difficulties in a love relationship— have you given it all up?

Question: No.

Angela: Because of the pain. You're not willing to give up love? Well, then why should you give up justice?

Question: I don't want to give it up; I want to figure out how to do it.

Angela: I think what Gloria said is so important, that the best way to do this work is not to think of it as something special, not to think of it as something that is different from our lives, but to think of it as a way of living our lives, that this is the way we must learn to live our lives.

Question: As a lesbian, I am really appalled at how much money and energy my community is spending in supporting so-called Hate Crimes Bills to make there be more vicious prison sentences for crimes against specific peoples, as if that's the answer. I'd like to hear what you think about that.

Mililani: When I was looking at the gender equity thing in Beijing there was a really big issue of struggle. When the *two-spirit* sisters came over to struggle with us on that issue, one of the things that they pointed out is that there is increasing violence because of their sexual orientation, and because of homophobia. It is just swept underneath the rug. But there are a lot more people, including people in the social justice and human rights movement, who are willing to talk about racial, hate crimes against Asians and all that. But they don't want to look at the violence against *two-spirits*, and that's why, when I came here to talk, I said we have to put this on the agenda. You have to talk openly about it.

I do want to say, though, during those days there were some women who did not want the term "gay" or "lesbian," but they wanted to be called by their indigenous name. So within that issue, there is now a cultural sub-issue, but I think the only way that we are going to really address homophobia, just like racism, is that we cannot just talk generally and when the budget time comes, we are going to address that. When we go to the Legislature to fight for money to keep our streets safe, we have to address this issue. There is no other way but head-on, take the bull by the horns, head-on.

María: I want to add that I hate in general the basic fear. And I think that fear has a context. I think that the context is the insecurity and anxiety produced by economic restructuring world-wide.

In the work that I do documenting human and civil rights abuse on the border, I have observed that increasing border enforcement creates ever greater risks for people who have no choice but to cross without documents. I've often argued that we will be continually treating the effect, which is what I think we do when we criminalize hate. We treat the effect. We're not dealing with the root causes. We don't address the issue of economic security and sustainable development for communities, in order to create a more positive form of addressing the fears and anxieties that are the basis for hate.

Angela: I was involved in some of the very early efforts to develop model legislation for laws against racist violence and then homophobic violence. I understand what you mean, the way the laws are often rendered very racist in their effects. Now, what do you do? Do you say, "Well, let's get rid of the laws?" Or do you recognize that laws themselves have never really brought about any change. It's the movement that people organize to demand that they be implemented in progressive ways, that creates change.

The fact is, the conservatives have the upper hand on this, and that is why, increasingly, hate crimes laws are being used in ways that are objectively racist. As a matter of fact, I'd be interested in seeing how many cases are being brought against people of color for committing hate crimes against white people, as well? This is what is happening; this is the way the laws are being used. However, if our movements become larger and more effective, then that will change the way the laws themselves affect our lives.

Question: I have more of a statement, but I do want to thank you all for coming to our community here and speaking.

The last time I saw Mother Earth there was just one world. I think we should say what it is we mean when we say First World, Third World—the exploited and the most exploited. I think we should stop using the concept of the First and Third Worlds. I would appreciate that.

Question: I would just like to ask all of you about privatization of public services. As far as I can tell, a deal is being cut on the highest levels—by the right wing, who want all the public services to be performed by churches or something like that—and the Democrats saying, "Okay, well, the state won't do the services anymore, we'll turn it over to private corporations." What are your thoughts on organizing against that?

María: I hope we already are organized. At least at different levels. Privatization is part of the politics of economic restructuring. It's indispensable to it, in terms of not only the United States. All over the world international financial arrangements are being created. And the problem is that privatization puts a greater burden, not just on churches, but on private sources. Primarily the burden will fall to the family unit. And when there is no access to health, no access to child care; it'll be probably other women—poor women, or low income individuals who will have to "privately" assume the responsibility of health care, and other human services— or simply go without.

This one of the areas where we do have to organize because we do have certain social responsibilities such as education and health. We need to coalesce in order to assert that public has a right to those public services.

Gloria: And I think there have been some instances of success with health cooperatives, people putting together their own health care facilities. Because there is no national health care, in some specific areas, cooperatively owned businesses have been created. Health Care Associates of the Bronx is nine-hundred women who give home health care. They cooperatively own the business. It's not about profit, it's about creating good jobs and good health care.

There are some ways that we can seize the initiative ourselves and invent different economic forms.

Question: I wanted to thank all of you also. I think that it's really important that there are elementary school children who can hear and see women in positions of power who are educating us.

One thing that you said, Gloria, during your speech, was to challenge each of us to meet four people and talk about what we cared about and what was important to us. Well, my friends and I here have decided to go beyond that and sort of meet all of you right now. My name is Leslie Byrdie.

Question: I'm Sharon Barnes, Hi. This is a call to action. Yes, you can consider this our call to action. We just have several things to announce to you.

In case you didn't know, Austin is a very activist-centered community. Both of us are involved with the Lesbian Avengers. Thank you!

I know that probably most of you have heard about the Chuy's Action that is supposed to take place tomorrow. We wanted to let you know that it has been canceled because a resolution was reached. So right on. Thank you, thank you.

Gloria: This young woman says she's a welfare mom, and they can get together and have the parade that Angela talked about.

Question: Hi, I'm Sam, *hi'ya*, guys, or women. Let's see, Angela, when you spoke, I was really intrigued by the description you gave of certain forms of sexism and racism mutating. And I was interested historically how you have watched these mutations. What I'm concerned with is that we may still be addressing these mutated forms of sexism, etc. in manners that I guess could be described as treating that new strain with the same old antibiotics— we're seeing things like— you're either for or against affirmative action, or you're either feminist or not, things like that.

The discussion seems to need to be broadened extremely—like with affirmative action, it seems that we need to have a broader dialogue to be able to describe more than inequity, more than disadvantage. I'm not sure what the new medication for these new strains of sexism and racism is.

Angela: I think you've said it very compellingly. The question is, how do you recognize the new forms? I wanted to suggest that criminalization now is a form of racialization. That's just one example. It's no longer necessary to attach race to the presence of crime. All you have to do is evoke it. Or evoke the figure of the criminal. The criminal is already figured as black or as Latino. You see what I'm saying? So this is racism that is leading a kind of camouflaged existence. It becomes difficult even to talk about that as racism precisely because race is not even explicitly evoked.

I wanted to suggest that we have to think about some of those new ways in which racism and sexism express themselves; that we don't necessarily acknowledge or recognize as racism or sexism. There's a book that you might be interested in reading by Michael Omi and Howard Winant and is called *"Racial Formation in the United States."* It looks historically at the way race and racial formations have changed. That might be helpful. Are you a student?

Question: No.

Angela: Well, maybe we'll get together and talk later. Maybe I'll give you my mail address, and we can talk about it.

Question: My question is for Mililani. Western feminism has pressed for access to birth control. I was wondering if you could comment on limits to reproduction, caps on birth in developing countries, if we can use that term.

Mililani: There are two things that I would say with regards to contraceptives and that is that we need to be aware that contraceptives generally have come out of the pharmaceutical industry. Their primary motivation is profit. When we look at the cause of breast cancer in our generation and our mother's generation, a lot of it is attributed to taking oral birth control pills that contained too many hormones, but nobody really cared because they were making a lot of money.

The other thing I wanted to say on that is that Norplant and

Depo-Provera are bad, bad, bad. Don't take them; women out there, look for another product.

These things are really being pushed, not only by American pharmaceuticals, but now the World Health Organization is sending them out globally.

With regards to the question of population control, and this is something that we took on in Cairo, the politics of population control are very subtle, and they require a great deal of inquiry.

I used to think, when I looked at population control programs, that they were good. I had this idea firmly implanted several years ago, when I was looking at the nature of my call for service, and I went to Calcutta to work with Mother Teresa and with people who were dying. If you have never seen what overpopulation is, then let me recommend that you work in Calcutta with Mother Teresa.

I talked with her about the abortion issue. And when I came to Cairo, I began to inform myself about the politics of population control and transfer, and one of the things that very much astounded me was that population control policies are developed by western nations and imposed on "underdeveloped" nations because there is a great tenacity on the part of western consuming industrialized nations and transnational corporations to seize control of natural resources that are rightfully the property of other peoples and other nations.

When you look at the politics of population control, there is a pattern. The consuming nations want control of populations on land bases that they have targeted for their own commercialization.

When I was in Beijing I was informed of this by panels of black women from Africa who were talking about population control policies.

We are raised to think that we have all kinds of population problems—places like Zimbabwe and Kenya and elsewhere. But really, they have much more acreage available per person, man, woman and child, than is available in the West.

If we're going to make sure that 6% of the population of the West is going to continue to control and consume 80% of the resources in what is called the Third World, then we have to control the populations of those places.

I'm not saying that overpopulation is not a global problem. I'm saying that when you attack that problem, you need to take a look at where the populations are that are being targeted; whether or not their land base and their traditional resources and economy are sufficient to support them. If the conclusion of that analysis in your mind is "Yes," then you need to be very cautious about supporting population control.

I think that we need to be more creative in looking for ways of contraception, and I can't say enough that Norplant and Depo Provero are bad for women. We've got to throw that stuff out, and insure at the same time that those products are not taken and dumped in Africa and Asia and Central and South America—which is also a practice we are struggling against.

Gloria: And I think that, as feminists, population control is not our phrase. That is their phrase. I would suggest that we never use it, because to the extent that language can change thought, if we always speak about reproductive freedom, it's very helpful, because it means the freedom to have children, as well as the freedom not to have children, and it gives the power to the individual to make the decision.

Question: Hi, this is less of a question and a huge invitation to everyone who is left in the room, specifically, to all of you, if you're still going to be in Austin tomorrow at noon, and specifically to the women who said, "How do I become an activist?"

We're going to have an action tomorrow at noon at the Mitsubishi dealership here in Austin. This has gotten no press in Austin, and very little, from what I can find, on the internet. This is a feminist issue and a human rights issue. This is a union issue. These are UAW workers; this is a corporate issue; this crosses all the borders that we've been talking about.

So I invite all of you to come at noon tomorrow for one hour of your day, if you can.

Question: Hi. I'm a 25-year old woman who just went back to school for the first time this year and have been struggling with the economic basis to go to school. I've done the service industry and found that last year when I became unemployed I could get a federal grant. This year I made $7,000, and that's $1,000 too much to go to school on a federal grant. I want to present to you a letter to the administration of Bill Clinton, which I faxed, telling him that anyone who thinks a person could live on $6,000 or less a year is pretty much into deprivation.

I want to know if you know of any other ways for students to get out of economic oppression. I've often heard about all sorts of grants and loans, but I've never seen them.

Gloria: I don't think any of us know why this crazy rule exists. There's probably a whole foundation library someplace, right? If you looked at all the possible—you've looked at the grants?

Question: I've looked under women, and under dyslexia, and I haven't found anything. How can a government fail to help students?

Gloria: We can all organize ourselves and lobby on that. But you know, in the meantime, think innovatively. I know somebody who sold, so to speak, shares in herself and got $500 per investor. She got herself through two years of graduate school by selling shares in herself. And she wasn't offering profit. She wasn't trying to run capitalism here on herself, she was just saying— I promise that I will do good in the world, and it will pay off in other ways. She writes to her investors and tells them what she's doing.

You know, sometimes, if we just try to think of something that hasn't been done before, rather than something that has been done before, we'll come up with something.

Angela: And you know, also in connection with that, because I'm still pushing this prisoner-student coalition possibility, and you know one of the things that the very government has done is to abolish grants for prisoners so that prisoners who used to be able to use grants to get college, university educations, while they were incarcerated can no longer do so. That's something you could start working on.

Gloria: You have a coalition issue right here. I see the coalition blooming.

Question: I was also hoping to explore the student-prisoner idea. I'm a student again who has been to jail, but there were also a lot of differences between me and the other women there. I was really glad that you used the word "fascism" because I think in order to keep getting profits, they're going to have to continue to take away our civil liberties and our rights. Basically, if things keep going the way they're going, we're all going to wind up in jail if we don't do anything. And so a working coalition with people who are now incarcerated is not an altruistic thing. It's a matter of "we are in that place."

I mean, I'm wondering, you've done so much work with prisoners, can you share possible models?

Angela: There are students who are doing work around prison issues. You can find interesting things on the internet. About a month ago, there was a nationwide action. The demand was, "Education, Not Incarceration," and students chained themselves to various sites and went on hunger strikes to demand that the proliferation of prisons stop. There's a whole group of students at Oberlin who started a group about three years ago. They have a lot of stuff on the worldwide web. There are students at UC-Santa Cruz, where I teach, who did an act of civil disobedience at Soledad Prison. They protested the expansion of Soledad and prevented the construction workers from doing the work. They all got arrested, of course, but it was a civil disobedience action, and they were expecting that. So there is a lot going on. There's a round table for women in prison that happens; it's national. There's a conference coming up. You know, we can talk about it, because there is a lot going on. But I think that these issues have to be integrated even more onto the agendas of all kinds of organizations, aside from the coalitional work between students and prisoners.

Gloria: There's no substitute for this collective action. There's also individual action. There are versions of the "Each one teach one" idea too, in which people, students go into a prison and find one or two or three prisoners who want to learn something the students know. Maybe it's computer skills, maybe it's what you're getting in your classroom, maybe it's access to particular books that you can get out of the library and get to them.

Angela: I did take students into prison, into a jail. I was teaching a course on incarcerated women and took ten students from the class at San Francisco State into the jail once a week. The students talked to prisoners. But first I insisted that the prisoners teach with the students. The students had to learn how to be taught by the prisoners before they could do that work. Otherwise, it would be missionary work.

Question: My name is C.C., and I'm from Chicago. I'm going to

UT-Austin. There's a concern among some activists that I've recently met about the right taking on the rhetoric of struggle—doing things like the Mitsubishi people are doing. They are paying people to demonstrate against the EEO office. I'm not really sure what's going on in California with the "Civil Rights Initiative." Is this something new, or have you all seen this before, and how did you all deal with it?

Gloria: No, it's not new. Think of the phrase makers. You know, "Right to Work" is anti-worker. "Right to Life" is not counting women's lives as lives. Hitler called his party "National Socialism." So the perversion of the language, the doublethink is always there. But the idea of paying people to demonstrate is different from taking over the language of struggle. You need to just expose it. It's not new. It's true, it drives you crazy, but you just have to keep exposing it.

Photo © Jane Steig Parsons, Prints Charming Photography

Feminist Family Values Essay and Art Contest

Winner: Susan Barber, Amherst, MA

Air drying laundry became a nationwide trend. Lovely things started happening. People paid more attention to the weather. They spent more time outside. People did fabulously creative things with their useless dryers. Celia's class made an aquarium and inspired a local Laundromat. In cities, where planting space is limited, neighborhoods got together and grew community gardens in their dryers.

It was amazing. As people were hanging their wash they began to imagine other ways of conserving energy. Across the nation people began to think beyond *paying* for their energy and wondered where it came from and what the *real* costs of its production were.

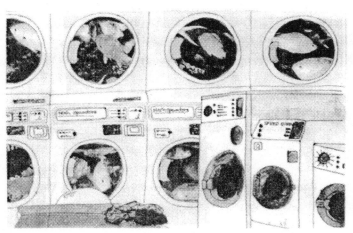

Social consciousness was raised. The population began to appreciate how everything was connected to everything was connected to everything. Celia just smiled to herself and eyed the dishwasher.

This excerpt from the winning children's story and art by Susan Barber is from a story entitled, *"Celia's Story: The End of the Dryers, or How the World Became a Better Place."* The organizing committee selected Susan's work because it captured the spirit of the Feminist Values Essay and Art Contest. The purpose was to promote feminist thought, provide information, and inspire movement based on hope. Susan Barber is a student at the Art School of Syracuse University in New York.

Finding Alternative Values: Introduction to the Community Program

Genevieve Vaughan

Founder, Foundation for a Compassionate Society

When I came back to the United States in 1983 after living in Italy for about twenty years, I brought an international perspective home with me. Rome is a place that all roads lead to, so people from all over the world were there. There were newspapers which served the different populations and political persuasions. Many widely different points of view were represented including a strong left wing perspective. At that time Italy had the largest Communist Party outside China and Russia. It is also the headquarters of the Catholic Church—which gives you the idea of the wide spectrum of political points of view which were 'mainstream' there.

I was in Italy during the Vietnam War and really felt how much Italian people were against it. I got an international perspective which made me see that our country was responsible for a lot of wrongdoing in the rest of the world. I came back here in 1983, convinced that I should do my political duty to make things better, not only for people inside this country, but for other people outside it as well.

I had become a feminist in Italy, and I really believed then, as I do now, that feminism is the way to make social change. In fact, feminism is wider than Marxism because there are more women on earth than there are industrial proletarians. I don't think that feminism has been taken seriously as a political philosophy, and it needs to be. In fact, as I have lived in this country, trying to create a foundation which acts according to women's values, or feminist values, I find the definition of reality excludes any alternative point of view. People are very much influenced by newspapers, television, and so forth, in which information is actually edited out and only some values are emphasized with the result that an alternative point of view is not allowed to come forward.

For example, in the United States we blame individuals for the problems that exist instead of blaming the system. In Italy I learned to look as things systemically. I would say that in the U.S. we have a system which we could call "Patriarchal Capitalism." Although it promotes itself and seems to be all-pervasive, we can, as feminists and as women, learn to find within ourselves the values that are alternative to it and we can unite in solidarity with each other.

In spite of its own congratulatory definitions of itself, the system of Patriarchal Capitalism is creating devastation for people all over the earth. It has evolved from the system of slavery to military and economic colonialism to what is now called "Free Market" economics. I think the word "free" there is really a red flag because it means "free rein for some people to exploit other people." That's actually the way it works; the few profit from the economic domination of the many. We as women and as feminists should not support a system where some people dominate and others have to submit, whether this is on a worldwide or on an individual scale. We have to be able to find alternative values and base a different system on them.

I went to the Women's Conference in Nairobi in 1985 and to the Women's Conference in Beijing in 1995, and I found that the women of the world really do have an alternative perspective already. There were 40,000 women in the village of Huairou in China. Among women from different countries, classes, races, religions, etc., there was a great deal of commonalty in opposing Patriarchal Capitalism and in finding creative, life enhancing solutions to the problems it causes. We were women from everywhere, trying to create a different world, starting each with her local area.

As we explore the subject of Feminist Family Values and the challenges facing our local communities, it is important for us in this country to see ourselves in the context of the international women's movement. Unfortunately, our consensus-forming media and political, academic and religious authorities do not usually allow us to see where we stand among our sisters or to know what our system is doing to them. We have to take the responsibility of informing ourselves and re-contextualizing ourselves among them, of reaching out of the dominator countries and categories to become allied with those who refuse to submit. We also have to refuse to submit to being bought out by the system, to being dispossessed of our point of view and our values, to being co-opted by the Prozac of privilege which makes us adapt to perpetrator values without protesting. The international women's movement sets the standard by which all women can find their truth and their common ground.

Photo © Jane Steig Parsons, Prints Charming Photography

Photo © Danna Byrom.

Introduction to the Community Speakers

María Limón, Poet and Writer

Foundation for a Compassionate Society

The forum's purpose is to give a voice to the many issues women face as they work to improve their lives, their families' lives, their communities' lives. I know, as Adrienne Rich says, that each of the women who are attending as speaker, and each of the participants, "holds a piece of my truth. My truth is incomplete until I have heard and learned their truth and your truth." Sexism teaches a lie that women cannot trust our intelligence, our passion and our strength. Society teaches that we are incapable of acting. It teaches us to wait for someone else to do the leading. The women sitting on this panel are women who no longer wait. They have seen problems, assessed strategies, and have acted decisively and creatively. They are women from Central Texas; they are the leaders that we have been waiting for. "We" are indeed the leaders we have been waiting for.

Editors Note: Selections from the transcripts of the community speakers have been chosen to create a sense of the vision and concerns of the community. The full proceedings are available on video tape from the Foundation for a Compassionate Society.

Photo © Jane Steig Parsons, Prints Charming Photography

Ana Sisnett

TecnoMama, Foundation for a Compassionate Society

I'm a poet, I'm an immigrant and I'm a parent of a son and daughter. I must say that given everything—from ignorance and lack of sensitivity and widespread deliberate attempts to discredit women in general, and feminism in particular—it is amazing that we can gather here to develop and work on strategies to implement the reflection of feminist perspectives.

Among the challenges to feminism that I have been most sensitive to is access to media—training, funding, equipment, extensive policies, studies, decision making, freedom of speech and expression, structures for implementation of those policies, legislation and strategies that are sensitive to the needs and interests of women and girls. Of course, essential to all these is spoken, signed and written literacy.

It is also critical we look at the way in which the creation of an infrastructure is needed to provide media resources, ecological integrity and labor conditions that assure physical and emotional health for workers.

While the work I do currently focuses on demystifying the Internet and advocating for greater inclusion for people who are traditionally left out of circles of power, I am well aware the Internet may not be appropriate for everyone. But it is up to each community to determine what is appropriate for them and in order to do that. They need to know what it is they are choosing to accept, or not.

We, as women, work with innumerable forms of technology, from beer and cheese making machines to highly developed technologies. Our work has led us to remind women they need not be embarrassed if they don't know how to work a machine. How many of us remember putting fax paper in backwards the first time, or remember hanging up when an answering machine took our first call?

We advocate for a multifaceted approach that includes radio, television, cable access, fax networks, print media, video and computer networking and any other form developed and promoted by the communities from which they arise. We promote collaboration, communication, information sharing and gathering. And we advocate for media women themselves to make room in the field of media work to include themselves in all facets of organizing and advocacy.

All too often we don't do the work of lobbying and advocacy on behalf of greater access to media by women. I urge all of us to notice and to remember that while we drag our feet on these issues, while we work to understand it, while we ponder over what all this is about, the right wing around the world and the fundamentalist forces have been extremely efficient at using all kinds of media to promote themselves and their agenda.

It is up to those of us with information to share it. I advocate that we put aside our resistance to, and fear of, the new and different, and that we learn about the ways technology affects our lives in order to better counter the dangerous effects of them on our lives.

Why not appropriate media for our best interest and for our communities? Why not have our own media, our own C-Span, our own CNN, our own radio stations to cover the institutions that are daily making decisions that affect our lives without our knowledge and without our participation.

It is not far-fetched, in my opinion, and given what I've seen around the world . . . when you consider the collective power of women.

Mary Ellen Curtin

Professor of History, Southwest Texas State University

The reality is that women must be able to take care of themselves and their children economically. Where are the movies about these issues. The persistence and dominance of the madonna/whore imagery in our popular culture, coupled with the myth of Prince Charming, speaks volumes about the inability of TV and movies to speak to us about the realities of women's lives and concerns.

As an educator, it is my job to introduce feminism to all of my students, male and female, but especially female, because they need feminism to make sense of the world around them and of their own lives.

bell hooks talks about the emotional and psychological cost black women pay for being black and female in this society. In an essay called "Healing Our Wounds, Liberatory Mental Health Care," she states:

"Currently, conventional mental health professionals who tend to the needs of black folks, often reject any analysis that takes into account a political understanding of our personal pain. This may be true of black mental health care workers as well as everyone else. While there is a growing body of self-help literature that is addressed specifically to black folks, it does not connect political injustice with psychological pain. For example, even though many self-help books for black folks look at the issue of low self-esteem expressed in extreme self-hatred, sometimes overtly relating it to internalized racism, such works rarely talk about healing processes that would include radical politicization and social activism."

I think hooks' words need to be thought about by everyone in our society who bears the weight of maintaining the capitalist—racist—patriarchal system. Poverty, racism, sexism all hurt. They all have immense psycological consequences that can potentially lead to self destructive behavior.

Dottie Curry

Community Outreach, Planned Parenthood

I seem to have been born into activism. . . remember standing up at school, church, at regular neighborhood places, fighting for the rights of disabled people, disadvantaged people, for myself, as a woman, for myself as a black person.

Down through the years it has been hard to separate my activism and my fighting for rights of people and my fighting for the rights of women, of the disabled, for mental health rights. And I think I have decided that it's not necessary. I think I fight for human rights, across the board.

Originally, I didn't know what I was doing was feminism, or activism. Then all of a sudden there was Gloria Steinem, and there was Angela Davis. There were people who were putting words to my suffering and my pain, my struggle. Also to my hopes and dreams. And that was a great comfort to me.

I think that is what I want to say to you. Whatever you are working for or against, don't do it alone.

I went to China to the International Women's Conference and I noticed that women all around the world are thinking the way I'm thinking and the way you're thinking. Having all those women there thinking about the rights of women together was incredibly powerful, as having all of you here today is powerful.

I was most fortunate to get married when I was very young, so I have my children, six of them, and grandchildren and great-grandchildren. I have my mom and my grandmother. I have firsthand knowledge of seven generations of women, so I can see how feminism has worked and the progress that has been made down through the years. When people say, "No progress has been made," I have to disagree with them. From the time of my grandmother—who was a first generation free black woman, to my great-granddaughter, who will have opportunities I never even dreamed were available—progress has been made.

There is also a fear that all this can be taken away, and for cultures like mine, a fear of putting things in writing, or on the internet. It's going to take time. So notice that, and give us a hand—no criticism please.

These are my thoughts: "Don't do it alone." "Know progress has been made." "As long as we hang in together, this world will be the kind of world that we want it to be, for women, and everybody."

Sharon Bridgforth

Root Wym'n Theater Company, writer/artistic director
HIV Outreach Specialist, Planned Parenthood

I never heard the word feminist
  growing up.

I was raised by independent, freedom/seeking wy'mn
that grew-up in the segregated south
twelve in a shack/grown they own food wy'mn
that helped raise the neighborhood children
sewed, ironed and cleaned ms. anne's house
cooked in the white only country clubs
taught at the coloured only schools/ and
loved me fiercely.

I never heard the word feminist
growing up and today I am angry
and I am hurt because in preparing for this dialogue
I realized that the privilege of
language/context and understanding of
what this society does to wy'mn
stayed in the whiteonly sections of town
therefore
I was denied the skills necessary
to defend myself in certain degrading
and heartbreaking situations.

I think that feminism
must meet the challenge of accessibility in the 90s . . .
racism-classism-elitism
must be disembodied from the movement   banji
girls/round the way homegirls, cholas, unruly
dykes, poor wy'mn, elder wy'mn, culturally
traditional wy'mn/and girls
need to be invited to the table
given their props
listened to
heard
and
taught!

I think feminists must organize educational programs
much like the HIV/AIDS activists did,
getting out in the community

standing on street corners
talking in churches and schools first
learning how to truly
embrace and appreciate
diverse populations.

I didn't hear the word feminist
growing up I hope that the
girl (& boy) children of the 90s
don't have to say the same.

Lillian Stevens

Esperanza Peace and Justice Center

Feminism is a particularly painful word for me. My first experiences with it grew out of my need for activism and my sense of political isolation. My attempt to find a place in the feminist movement was met by resistance from white women whose deeply entrenched fear of the color of my skin drove me into deeper isolation that I had known before.

Similarly, my first experience with black nationalism offered me a pre-defined space, subordinate to my African American brothers. I left and isolated myself again.

White male supremacist ideology is like a cancer. It has metastasized itself into sexism, racism, classism, heterosexualism and other forms of oppression that each by itself can make our society ill, but the singular elimination of one cannot make us well.

My first positive experience with feminism was in 1989. The organization was the Esperanza Peace and Justice Center in San Antonio, Texas. It is a women of color, feminist organization—anti-racist, anti-ageist, anti-classist. We are an AIDS activist and human rights activist organization that advocates for the rights of lesbians and gay men and provides a space for artists, environmentalists, animal rights advocacy and anti-war activism. Our space is a meeting space, a resource center and an art gallery.

It is my responsibility, as a woman who has walked away, to not be complacent with the work we are doing, but to engage in critical dialogue and yes, criticism—to not be the person who is always easy to get along with, but the one who is demanding and demanding and demanding—because, until we become proactive and devoutly engaged in eliminating white male supremacist ideology, our society is terminal.

Dr. Mercedes Lynn de Uriarte

Professor of Journalism, University of Texas

I am a woman and a mother. I have a son and a daughter. I was a single-head-of-household when I started college as a freshman and by the time I left graduate school, we were all three in college. Mine is a class trajectory as well as a personal history. Raised in upper middle-class Mexico, I lived the aspiring U.S. middle class experience until divorce introduced me to poverty.

Although I consider myself a feminist, I do so privately. I appreciate what feminists have done to open access to women, but I have never been able to identify with the movement, in part because I have never found it to be very welcoming of diversity. In fact, I find it to be narrow in class perspective and concerns.

One of my concerns with the women's movement has been its low profile value of nurture—both in the family and in the workplace. Within the women's movement, the values most promoted seem to be those associated with career advancement. Gone are the days when women talked about feminizing the workplace and making it a less driven, more nurturing environment. Instead we seem to support beating the men at their own game.

We do not, as a women's movement, seem to value family nurture either. We do not seem to question whether the early assignment of children to child care facilities is a form of buying the liberation of one generation at the expense of the next. Never have we asked as a movement, if our children are regimented from the age of six-months, from whence will come the next generation's rebels?

Beyond that, the movement has not recognized that diversity implies differing family values. For many cultures, closeness to one's family, daily interaction with one's children is every bit as important as earning money.

The women's movement is not just myopic in terms of culture and values, but in terms of class as well. Thus its goals tend to be set with the assumption of middle-class position or above. As a result, it cannot understand that for many minority feminists, jobs for men are a feminist issue. They lead to stability in the family. Work for our sons and lovers is as important as work for our daughters. Almost 50% of minority children live in poverty. That is a feminist issue— or should be.

Today almost half of the nation's wealth is owned by 1% of the population; 20% of Americans own 80% of the nation's wealth. That means 80% of us are trying to get by on the remaining 20%. Add to that fact that women bear the brunt of U.S. poverty. That makes class a feminist issue. But it's not very well explored by the women's movement, especially in regard to minority women.

Another reason that I find it hard to identify with the women's movement is because of its selfishness. Affirmative action is a case in point. Feminists have been basically quiet while media has defined affirmative action as something that effects minorities. Nevertheless, white women, according to all studies have benefited more from affirmative action that minority women. Once on the profesisonal career track, white women have not advocated effectively for minority inclusion. Indeed, in the academy, the position of minority women has not changed in twenty years according to studies published last year in the *"Chronicle of Higher Education."*

In journalism white women make up 50% of all the journalism academics in the country, but minorities, men and women together, make up about 2%. There are twenty-four Latinos, men and women, nationwide. Six of us are women.

So while it is critical that we continue to fight for access, as that access gets labeled negatively, white women seem to be very quiet and that is hard to understand unless this is a white women's movement.

The role of the press affects the lives of each of us regardless of our field or identity. The women's movement has suffered its own bruises at the hands of a press that would rather promote images of bra-burning than explain complex social issues. But then the press is a male dominated field. Indeed, it is now in the process of consolidating even more rigidly that situation. Two years ago, eleven women editors were among the editors of 1,600 daily newspapers in this nation. Since then, corporate push-out maneuvers have lowered that figure to eight.

Consolidation is part of an overall pell-mell U.S. corporatization of media that warrants serious concern. Media defines us, defines for us, while historically and currently it denies us voice, disallows us to speak on our own behalf, through our own perspectives. Indeed, the Time Warner, Disney, CNN merger concentrates almost more than half of these media enterprises in international communications.

Today 14 companies control more than half of the daily newspaper business. At the end of World War II, daily newspapers received $1 billion a year in advertising. In 1992, those receipts totaled $32 billion. As wealth, decision-making and ownership concentrate, disinformation campaigns so evident in the past, could become even more effective in the future. "The disappearance from the world scene of a structured opposition to the global market economy also reinforces immeasurable the antisocial impulses being assiduously promoted." (Herb Schiller, media scholar) Given these factors, there is cause for concern that we face an era of corporate authoritarianism.

Meanwhile, what is the press worker profile? Consider the print press: 90% of all journalists are white, the majority are male. 7% are African-American, about 2% are Latino, 1% are Asian-American and less than .03% are American Indian. The smallest percentage within these statistics are the females. When has the women's movement expressed dismay at these profiles?

Given the lack of participation by minorities, it is little wonder that studies consistently indicate that minority populations are portrayed in predominantly negative terms and/or criminalized. These practices violate established codes of press ethics, but they are ignored with little concern. So when did the women's movement last organize over press portrayal of minorities? Of welfare mothers? Of minority youngsters who only appear in the press as gang members?

Historically, the contemporary women's movement has been unable to effectively express solidarity across cultural and class lines—let alone incorporate values that address minority concerns and definitions. We need to recognize the shapes that power takes, including white female power, and learn how to be feminist in both nurturing and activist ways.

Andrea Beckham

Choreographer, Dancer

I am a choreographer and dancer in this community and in the global community as well. In one of my first pieces I used a quote by Rebecca West that went something like this: "I don't know what a feminist is, but that's what they call me when I try to distinguish myself from a doormat or a prostitute."

I think there is art in everything we do everyday and that art should provoke and empower the audience.

My background is in Sociology. I was a Sociology major who had to dance.

I would like to encourage each and every one of you to dream huge, and then go out and do it.

Stephanie Thomas

Disability Rights Activist, ADAPT

In contrast to one of the earlier speakers, I was glad to see the title for this meeting, "Feminist Family Values," because I think the right wing has tried to monopolize the term, has tried to steal it from the rest of our society. I think the only way we can fight that is by taking back the idea that family includes us. If I had one goal for the feminist movement it would be to broaden our views of feminism.

If you look around you, at the panel and at the people beside you in the audience, you will see there are many other people here than the traditional white, middle-class, able-bodied women with whom feminism is so often equated.

I came to talk about women with disabilities and feminism, the many parallels between these two movements, how you can look at many issues and see that they have a disability part of them. I want to point to the relationship, for example, between reproductive rights and sterilization of people with disabilities because "we wouldn't want those people reproducing." I want to talk about economic rights. African American disabled women make twelve cents for every dollar that white able-bodied men make and there is a 75% unemployment rate among people with disabilities. I want to talk about domestic partnerships among disabled people who can't get a job or afford to get married because they would lose a third of their benefits. I want to relate gang violence to disabled issues. We hear about people being killed by gangs. Well, everybody doesn't die. A lot of them become disabled.

I could go on and on, but I have to talk about another issue first because it is fundamental to having people with disabilities involved in any other movement—accessibility. I'm really tired of talking about it, frankly, but it continues to be an issue. If you don't have access, people with disabilities cannot be part of what is going on.

Access is a civil right. People have gone to jail for that right, including me, and we will go again if we have to. And the women's movement is not exempt from that. There is no interpreter for the deaf here today. And when groups like Planned Parenthood tell us they don't have to have a clinic accessible because there is another one across town that we can get into, that's wrong. When they ask people with cerebral palsy why they need birth control, that's wrong. Access is not a thrill; it's a fundamental issue.

Another very important issue is long-term care. We need more community-based services so that people with disabilities don't have to be locked away to get the services they need. This is a women's issue if there ever was one. 75% of the people in nursing homes are women, older women. More than 60% of the primary paid caretakers are women. 90% of the unpaid caregivers are the mothers, daughters and wives of people who are disabled.

It is a women's issue, and if you wonder why it gets such low priority in the federal government and in our society, think about the fact that it really is a women's issue. There is a very strong institutional bias in the support services for disabled people for long-term care services. We spend six times as much money institutionalizing people in nursing homes and "state" schools (which are schools we never graduate from) as we do on community-based services, which enable personal freedom.

Every state that gets Medicaid is required to have a nursing home program. There is no requirement for community-based services. The lives of people with disabilities are basically not valued. That is something that feminism has looked at quite a bit. Democrats and Republicans are posturing. Nobody is willing to have the vision that maybe people with disabilities could live in their own homes for less money than we're spending now.

"Managed Care" is the idea of managing people with disabilities out the door of the entire system. And the ultimate expression of that is what Dr. Korvorkian does. The one right people with disabilities are promoted as having is the right to die. Physician-assisted suicide is the ultimate expression of the idea that it's better to be dead than disabled.

In your thinking about feminist family values, you need to think wide and work hard.

D'An Anders

Texas Council on Family Violence

I am an advocate for battered women and their children. I'm also an activist in the Democratic Party, dysfunctional as it is.

I have been a soldier in the war on poverty; I have done peace marches; I have done civil rights marches; I was a soldier in the sexual revolution. I'm tired of fighting these things. There was a time in my life when I thought Roe v. Wade settled reproductive rights issues. I was wrong. It is 1996 and I still send money and go to marches to get the minimum wage up to $5.25 an hour. I work every day to ensure that children who live in homes where violence is everywhere, when the divorce comes, don't get sent to live with the batterer.

Folks, there is something wrong with this picture.

I would present to you the suggestion this afternoon that all these problems are class based. Once the dominant paragon can divide us by race, the victory is theirs. You can take whatever issue you want and claim it as yours, but when you peel it back and you look down at it, the problem is all this division done by class. It you're at the top, fine. If you're at the bottom, that's just too damn bad. For every six who are trying to make it to the top, they'll let one up. And that makes another division.

The problem is not to worry about your share of the pie. The problem is to make the pie bigger. The answers to these questions are in your hands. You will have to fight these problems today, tomorrow and next week.

I suggest to you that it is a great honor and a great privilege to do so.

Anna Belle Burleson

Texas Council on Family Violence

I'm program director of the National Domestic Violence Hotline. I'm a survivor of domestic violence and I'm a single mom.

Everyone, everyone—men, women and children—deserves, has the right as a human being, to live in a safe home. Our homes should not be more dangerous than the street. We all have the human right, the civil right, to feel safe and secure when we are inside our homes. And battered women and children do not get that.

We hear a lot in the family values of the mainstream about how children need both parents. Well, that's not always true. When one parent is abusive, they lose their rights as a parent. Nurturing of children does not include abuse—physical, mental or verbal. And witnessing abuse is also a form of abuse.

One of the problems battered women face is a judicial system that continues to ignore the fact that violence needs to be taken into account when considering custody and visitation issues. Our judicial system and our entire society needs to stop blaming the victims; stop blaming the women and children who are being beaten and abused for the violence that happens to them.

Another problem that faces battered women is access to services.

There are many communities that don't have domestic violence shelters or programs where battered women and children can go. Even in communities where these services exist, often doors are closed on the basis of race, language, chemical dependency or disability.

The purpose of the National Hotline is to help battered women locate services. I believe every women who leaves a batterer, who calls the hotline, who steps into a shelter—joins our revolution whether she knows it or not. And we need to welcome her with open arms.

Finally, I want to challenge you to remember that domestic violence is everybody's business. Get involved.

Moira Dolan

Physician

Our apparatus to fight epidemics is medically termed the immune system. Immunity derives from a Latin word that translates as "exempt from public service." The defense system that is mobilized by microbial invasion, called our "immune response," demonstrates itself as an exclusionary model, and follows precisely along the lines of the military responses so characteristic of the dominant culture. Could it be that the reason our immune systems are increasingly ineffective is that we are in a global, furious race to avoid public service?

I suggest that the war on cancer, the war on AIDS, all these wars are only going to beget more wars, each more deadly than the last. To be successful organisms we need to have a new model of survival, as the old one, immunity, is clearly failing us. We do not need to keep protecting ourselves from each other's bodily fluids. We need an inclusionary model at the DNA level, a feminist model.

Today I propose an alternate archetype, that of community: an inclusionary model among feminist principles. What this means on a subcellular level is already evidenced in the case of drug-resistant bacteria. These little microbes have successfully deflected the threat of modern medicine's biggest gun antibiotics by opening up their genetic material to include a little scrap of gene from a virus. That piece, or plasmid, codes for the bacteria's antibiotic resistance.

Perhaps we can only discover under the microscope that which we have already imagined in our dreams. And so I invite you to share the visions I have been receiving in my meditations: DNA unwinding to allow the inclusion of viral genetic material. Our goal is the development of a new, resilient DNA based on a community model.

This is deep (subcellular) feminism.

Candra Gaither

Planned Parenthood

The first time I heard the word "feminist" I remember thinking instantly of my mother and all the great work that she did, that she's always been a feminist.

She's never told me stories about marching, or going to jail and she certainly doesn't have stories about whom she heard speak or went to see. But she always worked hard and she has always been a stronghold for me. I certainly stand on her shoulders and am ready to move on. But one thing I've always noticed about her is that she keeps it on an everyday level.

I can think of eighteen problems and one small solution: I want you to start appreciating the women around you and the good work they do.

And start with your mom. Moms are such funny things, because sometimes you like to think they're not feminists—uh-uh, they didn't do this or that—they did. They did everything. They worked hard, and they raised you, and that's hard work. And start there, start appreciating what they do.

Sometimes I drop in on my mom, just to help her out in her classroom, and I'm just amazed at this brilliant woman. She's working with children. This is perfect, you know, and I have to remember that. Start with your sisters. Start with your daughters. Start with your co-workers.

It wasn't a decision for us to be divided, but it's a decision for us to come together again, or for us to appreciate each other and support each other. Start when you go into the workplace Monday, because it's all going to come down to women having support from other women.

Carol Joseph

Social Worker

My name is Carol Joseph. I am a local social worker at an alternative school. I am a mother of a 17-year-old daughter. I am of Arab heritage. I'm a veteran of the United States Army, which is how I became a social worker, because if I hadn't had the G.I. Bill, I never would have thought about going to school.

I feel deeply privileged and inspired by everything that every woman has said here. I think that it's a privilege for us to be here today. There are many women who, right now while we're here, work 8:00 to 5:00 jobs. They can't be here because they can't leave their job today. They need the money, as little as it usually is. And for each one of us to be here, we do have a certain amount of privilege. And I encourage everyone to be thankful, to gain whatever privilege you can and to use every little bit of it that you eke out of the system to fight for privileges for other women.

I think that as feminists we need to be involved in unions. We need to either join unions, start unions, support women, and men, who are in unions; do whatever it takes so that workers in our country are fairly compensated for the work they do, that they have opportunities to come to things like this during the day. Basically we've been taught the women's movement and labor unions are separate issues. They're not separate at all. The fight for seeing that people are treated fairly and justly in their workplaces is the fight for women's rights.

Schakti Miller

Natural Health Practitioner

I grew up in a household with a mother who is a public health nurse whose specialty was maternal and child health. One of the things I remember my mother talking about was how difficult it was to be a nurse and be subservient to the male doctors. When it came time for me to choose to go to school, everything in my life was lined up to become a nurse. And I couldn't do it.

I could not be a person to do injections; it did not seem right to me, it seemed violent. Over the course of the next ten years or so, as I studied anthropology and world religion, I began to come up with my own ideas that have taken maybe another twenty years to formulate, and that's a part of what I want to share with you today. Health is a feminist issue.

It seems to me that the challenge facing all of us is to come up with a new paradigm. We live in a paradigm that is based on Newtonian physics that says we're all separate; it's a very mechanistic view, like a clockwork view, where there are different pieces, but they're not related to each other.

This is not true, and it's causing us to die.

What we need is a new paradigm that supports life, that supports interconnectedness, that is a feminine perspective. Feminine energy has to do with cooperation, power from within, partnership, long term goals for the collective benefit.

We need to work from a health model that says we can work with this body, not control it. Feminine energy has to do with nurturing, intuition, support, collective goals for the long term good of the community, connection to spirit and co-creatorship with life force. We are all facing extinction on this planet. We are killing the planet.

Denegrative disease is too common. It shouldn't be that way. There is too much toxcidity. Information is surpressed. It is against the law to tell people what they can do to help themselves. Doesn't that seem strange? Women for milllinea have been healers, this is natural and it is suppressed. We aren't by law allowed to tell each other what will work. I think it is part of a paradigm that says we need power over the masses and it keeps people from having power over their own healing.

Jude Filler

Texas Alliance for Human Needs

If we are so smart why are we behind the curve? We are many wonderful people working very hard, but we aren't unified. We are not honest always among ourselves. Among ourselves we have disagreed today a number of times and that's just natural and human. But somehow, if we are to achieve those goals we consider important, be it health for our children, security in our own old age, an end to the fear of war and human-made disaster, we will have to be organized.

I think the main reason we have failed is that the problem grows faster than we do. We're not really failing, it just looks like it. If the problem would stay static, we would be basking. But it is growing exponentially.

I recently talked to some of my students who chose to work for the Texas Alliance for Human Needs. I assumed they were feminists. To a person, they said they weren't feminists—but that they believed in everything feminist.

We have a problem. Our lingo has been co-opted. This wonderful word that goes back several centuries . . . that was conceived as a beautiful thing, the idea that things we think of as good about humans which are female . . . we are a gender planet . . . Earth is a planet of people with gender identities that make things happen . . . it also makes a heck of a mess when it gets out of balance . . . and it is out of balance now . . . somehow the word that defined the search for balance has been turned against us. I find that very sad.

I've decided we need to change that word. In the future when we refer to ourselves we should use popular words—like cheerleader. Katie Lee Gifford is the most popular woman in America. Maybe we could become the Kathie Lee movement instead of feminists.

The other team not only steals our rhetoric, but they've managed to make us look strange, even to our own children, the activists of the day, the ones who are concerned about cleaning the environment, cleaning the air, raising healthy children, coming up with good ways for people to be fed and sheltered. But they don't like the word feminist.

I think poetry and humor may be the only way we're going to get out of this.

Melissa García

Public Policy Graduate Student
LBJ School of Public Affairs

I see my life experience as one large experiment in feminist pedagogy. I was raised in a single parent home, within a large Latino family that was predominantly female, I went to a girl's high school and graduated from Sarah Lawrence College which is a bastion of feminist thought. I am at LBJ in a class that is 70% women. I am writing a thesis on the history of the Mexican feminist movement. Now I work for Latino USA, staffed by women primarily and headed by women.

Based on my experiences in these feminist camps I think there are various challenges to feminism in the U.S. There are two problem areas in particular. One is the ineffectiveness of the movement itself to create real change in the political realm. The second issue is the deviseness and division in the movement itself.

Within the last ten years there has been a shift in the movement from a political movement to an academic exercise. Academics enjoy an important place in the movement, give us a written history and educate the youth to be a kinder and more gentle society. But in the end we have become too one-sided. We reflect and ponder too much and act too little.

As a movement we have been crisis oriented. Only during heated debates do we get media attention—abortion, Roe v. Wade. We need to mobilize another mass movement. We are not a mass movement any more. We need to help girls grow up and not think they are post-feminist.

The movement has always defined itself as separatist, from other leftist causes. Issues of race and class have been subsumed under larger issues of gender. But positively, we're beginning to re-define this universalized concept of sisterhood and have learned to see how interconnected issues come together-race, class, gender, sexual orientation, disability.

We have women of color writing their own stories, various types of feminism have emerged. We work too often separately. We need to find a common thread.

Sonia Inge

LBJ School of Public Affairs
Women's Issues Network

I just want to make some requests. When you invite a woman of color to a panel, don't just invite one. When you ask for my help remember the manners your parents taught you—say please and thank you. When I tell you my interests are in trade and commerce and that I would like to work for the White House, don't call me an Oreo. I'm not a sell out.

I can be open to your ideas, I can be easy to please. And I can help you do what you want to do. Those are my requests. Peace, love and progress.

Marta Cotera

Chicana Historian

I agree and disagree with the term "family values." It sticks in my throat because of how it has been co-opted. But I will not let people take my words away from me. I want to call myself a feminist. I wrote a book about Chicana Feminists twenty years ago and I can't now say, "I made a mistake. I'm really a Chicana cheerleader."

I have been a political activist for a long time—civil rights work, chicano rights work, a founder of the Raza Unida party—which finally flushed the Republicans out of the Democratic party.

I was brought kicking and screaming into the Texas Feminist movement during the ERA (Equal Rights Ammendment) organization campaign. We organized 600 chicana votes for the ERA ballot, our people were the workers, their people were the cheerleaders. That's just one experience. Not one member of the committee would pay for their own committee. But I don't want to talk about that. I don't think those were feminists. They were opportunists.

Now we need to do re-approachment again. We're moving into a global, corporate fascist state. We really can't afford to nit-pick.

We need to look at the best strategies for organizing. Women of color have always told the feminist movement that they don't have to represent all our issues. Educated Latino women have 91% involvement in their communities. Uneducated Latino women have 85% involvement. That is 25% higher than other women in this country. We're not asking anyone to do our work. What we have asked for the last twenty years is to coalese. The problem has been sharing credit for accomplishments with women of color.

The only people who can protect our communities from this global, corporate fascism that is invading the world, will be the women, when we can make time from washing the dishes. You say, "What keeps women from doing more?" We have to do that second shift.

We need to start with coalition building, working with local groups, to work with teachers, high tech communities, working with all kinds of networks. We need to be very concerned with racism and affirmative action.

We do face a resurgence of civil rights problems. We, as feminists of color, need to go back and re-educate our communities about feminism to combat the surge of machismo nationalism that is on the rise.

Elizabeth (B.J.) Fernea

Writer, Filmmaker
Department of English and Middle Eastern Studies
University of Texas at Austin

I would like to discuss cross-cultural feminist issues today. I'm concerned with how American feminists are perceived by women in other parts of the world, particularly women in the Middle East, which is my area of expertise. Do we deserve our reputation?

I ask myself this question, as I have just returned from seven months of travel and interviewing women for my new book, *"In Search of Islamic Feminism,"* which is under contract with Anchor Press—Doubleday. I had resisted this project for many years because I thought it would be done by a Muslim woman.

I am writing the book from a very vulnerable position—as an American feminist. Maybe what Middle Eastern women think about us may offer clues about why many of my students don't want to be called feminists though they are working for many of the same goals as all of us.

Feminism has a bad reputation in the Middle East. Here are some of they ways some people have described it to me in the last year.

"Feminism is a lot of talk and no action."

"Feminism is like fast food. All flash, no nutrients."

"Feminism, is a western product. It may mean something to the women of America, but it doesn't mean anything to me. It doesn't speak to me."

"Feminism is designed to destroy femininity. All American feminists want to do is imitate men. If you are so against men in the United States, why do you imitate them?"

I answered, *"Because they have power."*

"Well," she said, *"If you're such a strong feminist, why don't you create your own sources of power? That's what we've been doing for 2000 years, but nobody noticed."*

"American feminists only represent the rich elites, not poor women."

"American feminists are not religious. They don't care about religion. They make fun of us because we are Christian, or Muslim or Jewish."

"You only care about the way we dress. You're obsessed with the veil.

We're not. We're not forced to wear the veil. Is the veil more important to me than a good job or food on the table?"

"American feminism focuses on women as individuals, as lone figures in a landscape, not as members of groups."

"American feminists only care about their own individual lot, they don't care about kids and husbands and old people."

When I defend the American feminist movement, I often get the following response. *"OK, you do it your way. But what has it got you? Do you get equal pay for equal work? Paid maternity leave?"* (Six months is the average paid maternity leave in the Middle East) *"Political and legal power in the top ranks?"*

We have to examine our own goals and see whether their criticisms are valid or not. We have to understand that feminist movements develop differently in different societies.

One woman in Kuwait said to me, *"You take an Arab woman and an American woman and put them down in the same social and economic circumstances, and guess who will survive? Not the American woman."*

I asked, *"Why?"*

And she said, *"Because the Arab woman is stronger. She has had to struggle all her life, and she's still alive."*

I answered that we prefer not to suffer just for the sake of suffering, like our mothers and our grandmothers did.

"I understand," she said. *"We don't want to, either. But we need to figure it out ourselves, based on our own experiences."*

And that is my final point. Many American feminists really, sincerely believe that we have the best country in the world, the best women's movement in the world. And that may indeed be true. But it is rude and arrogant to suggest that our way is right for everyone.

Tammy Goméz

Poet
Announcer, KO-OP Radio

"It is possible to speak too English. So literal that I offend the silent

language of averting eyes. It is possible to crack the air with whipping words that penetrate proud, quiet pockets of denial. So I mutter, mumble, stammer. Mutter, mumble, stammer. Mutter, mumble, stammer, hoping that your discriminating ears will be deaf to the words, so that somehow their intended meaning will enter a realm of acceptance in the stubborn caverns of unslit darkness that I want to illuminate for you. And for me."

Thank you.

I have, in the many years now that I've been presenting poetry and other thoughtful words to many kinds of audiences, come to value and respect the inner knowing and wisdom of all of us. I have moved on from being a lone speaker at a microphone at poetry readings to doing community media work, specifically with KO-OP Radio here in Austin, which is, as you may well know, a cooperatively-owned-and-run community radio station.

That is one of the solutions or avenues of hope I want to offer women who live in this community, many of whom I know or have worked with, many of whom have been guests on radio shows we have conducted.

We need not feel that this program today is the only time to share and hear and speak. There are media outlets in this community to serve you. I exhort you and invite you with deep, deep respect to come and participate in our programming.

I've come to recognize some challenges to feminism in this community. I think a lot of the other women here have addressed a kind of anti-coalition sentiment which may be an inadvertent or, in some cases, may be deliberate. I'm not one to judge or decide that for all of us, but I think it's important to recognize that there are forces, some of them maybe trickle down from a patriarchal system which penetrates Austin. Or maybe it's some of our own doing—to act *against* each other, or at least wholeheartedly not *with* each other. I think that is something that is regrettable.

I think that there is a lot of internalized racism, classism, and maybe even sexism in terms of homophobic sentiments that even the most outspoken and resilient, stalwart defendants of feminism have inside, that we have to address and we have to recognize.

We have to look at the systems and the institutions in place that degrade our attempts to unite and coalesce. Those institutions are racist, classist and sexist in nature. Women support them or are in collusion with them as much as men. We have to acknowledge it, excise it, work with it. Do your Taoist, Tai Chi internal breathing techniques, speak with others, whatever we can do, we have to do.

Listen to others, and when you feel the pain, the pain of your own internalized -isms, and the pain of seeing what those -isms and oppressions do to others, sit with that pain, know it, and from that, the flower will bloom. There is hope there, hope and a solution can spring from there. Thank you very much.

Yana Mintoff Bland, Ph.D.

Environmental Economist,
Foundation for a Compassionate Society
Association of Women of the Mediterranean Region

Happy Mother's Day, everyone!

I'm of Maltese, which is mostly Arabic, background. I'm really pleased with the variety of definitions of feminism today. I have never called myself a feminist because of some of the reasons that Elizabeth (B. J.) Fernea has outlined, and especially because feminists have not prioritized ending militarism and imperialism. Also, I always felt I was too feminine, too family-focused because what matters to me most is my family, my children, my love partner, my mother, my father, my hundreds of cousins, and all the plants and animals—because if we have the true definition of family, the biological definition is the whole community of life, of plants and animals too.

My son told me the other day that in school they all call me the Lehigh Lady because I have joined residents protesting hazardous emissions from the Texas Lehigh Cement Kiln. Lead, arsenic, benzene emissions are molesting our children. This isn't a rabid feminist making the analogy between military or industrial polluters and child molesters. I am just telling you what they do: they retard and dull the mental sagacity of our offspring; they cause unusual anxieties and hyperactivity among children. Increased juvenile violence has recently been linked to lead emissions. They retard the immune system and change normal hormonal development and functioning. There are 3,000 children within two miles of that plant.

I submit to you that feminists should realize that we have no immunity without community action.

We are looking for volunteers to help us with a community health study for the people who live around Kelly Air Force Base. They have millions of dollars to clean up the base and the surrounding neighborhood, but instead of doing what the community wants—very basic things like a $20 soil sample to see if there's lead in the soil where the children are playing—they have these high-faluting plans to bring down contractors from Oak Ridge and spend millions on these new techniques to decontaminate the soil with radio waves. How can we make these people accountable, how can we prove that the health of the neighborhood is compromised by their contaminants, by the shallow ground water being totally contaminated with benzene, chlorobenzene, perchlorobenzene, TCPs.

Jet fuel tanks are only a few hundred yards from where people live. There have been many spills, there was a spill just a week ago. Jet fuel has lead in it, it's not like other gasolines, so it's more toxic, has more toxic effects than even the Austin tank farm that was closed down through the actions of PODER in the community five years ago.

Help us demand immediate clean-up of the soil and ground water and air contamination, compensation for lost property values, compensation for health values, free medical assistance to victims, and a green buffer zone between Kelly Air Force Base and the community.

If I've taken two minutes to get this far, the U.S.Government has spent $2.5 million on the military in that time.

I want to end with our main demand, which I hope will become a main demand of the women's movement in the West, because it is a main demand of most women in the world, and that is that we unite and de-nuclearize and de-militarize the planet. Thanks very much.

Sylvia Herrera

PODER, *People Organized in Defense of Earth and Her Resources*
Health Researcher, Health Organizer, Health Activist

One of the things that unites us is that we're all survivors here, either of racism, sexism or classism. I would like to look at the word "survivor" in Spanish, "*sobrevivir*," means "to survive." But if you look at the literal meaning, it's "beyond living," beyond all the things that you've had to confront.

Other words come to mind. One is respect. I think that if we look at "respect," especially respect for women from other cultures, other groups, other groups with other different languages, then we can begin to dialogue.

Language is important, words are important. I challenge you to look at a language other than your primary language, because when you do that, you begin to develop the skill of listening. I think we've lost that, that we're not paying attention to each other or listening to each other. And we are not careful of what we say.

For instance, a lot of times, you hear people say, "Americans." Well, "*America es un continente, no un solo pais*," which means "*it's a continent, it's not just one country*." People are from the Untied States, but there are other countries that are in the Americas.

You hear the word, "Third World." Well, as my "*compañera*" Susana says, there is only one world. There are not several worlds here, and we're talking about Mother Earth.

After we develop respect we can begin to look at how other people have defined what family is, what values are.

As a Chicana from the East Side, my view of family is the extended family. We also have people who come into our lives but are not necessarily related but who still have titles like "*tia politica,*" I mean, where did that come from? "*Politica*" is politics, but the word is used for someone in your family. The other one is a "*madrina*" or "*padrino,*" godmother, godfather. Words are important.

I have extended family to my friends who give me support with my children, other women with children. We share our experiences.

That again is a redefinition of what and who families are.

And then from there, family extends to a group of women who have taken on a life commitment to women's rights, to Chicano rights, to basic human rights. That's a challenge. People say, "I'm in school," or "I'm doing this or I'm doing that." We've been able to keep that balance. You have to have that balance. We need to do it on a daily basis, making that commitment to making this a better world so that we can achieve basic human rights.

María Loya

PODER, People Organized in Defense of Earth and Her Resources.

As a young Chicana activist, I try to reflect on the past movements, past struggles, and one thing that I have recognized is that women have been the backbone of all movements of struggle.

We are the ones who get things done, we are the ones that organize fund raisers, call people up, rally people to go to events. And while we have been doing all the footwork, we haven't been getting the recognition. Press conferences, rallies, speeches have been done by men. In most cases this has not changed.

I had one person tell me that it was strange, that I was surprisingly outspoken, for a woman, a Chicana. I said, "Why is that strange to you?"

I realize when I talk to my sisters that we have a lot of opinions; but in many cases we have to recognize the dynamics that make us feel comfortable voicing those opinions.

What we have to do is provide support for young women so they can feel comfortable and confident, so they can realize their opinions are worth something. They have to step out from behind and get on the forefront, and get the recognition that they deserve.

We need to go beyond having classes at the universities about women's rights, because, in reality, most people don't go to universities. We're totally leaving a big part of a population of women out of this, out of this leadership training, out of this training to become more confident about public speaking.

Where are all the women from the barrio today? Where are all the women who are constantly fighting economic oppression and racist oppression that exists in the barrios. Where are these women, the fighters? Why aren't they here? Do we give them a forum so they can speak out? No, we don't. Because we don't consider them "legitimate" women leaders, we don't include them in the forum.

We have to think about that, and I hope you do think about not only women's rights within the white community, but women's rights everywhere.

Susana Almanza

PODER, *People Organized in Defense of Earth and Her Resources*.

I'd like to state that at one time we were all sisters and brothers, and the sky and the earth were our elders, and the parents were our leaders, and justice was our guide.

I've never belonged to what they say is the feminist movement. I can say "woman" and *"mujer"* but my tongue gets twisted with "feminist" and *"feminista."* Because of my indigenous ways, I've always been taught the strength is *"la familia,"* the family—that's the real strength, it's not whether you are woman or man, because we know there has to be a balance.

Justice has to be the guide. That is the indigenous way, that is the way we all had at one time. Justice was our guide and justice must continue to be our guide. Whether it's happening to a man or to a woman, to children, or to Mother Earth, Father Sun, justice has to be the guide.

We now see there is a hole in the ozone, which is the aura of Mother Earth. It has been penetrated by chemicals that are unnatural, that have remained there within the earth such a long time unmolested for a reason—because they were not to be moved, they were not to be let out, because of the harm that it could cause.

There's a hole in our aura too, and we're walking around all imbalanced here. We've got all of these negative thoughts —that is a woman of color, and that is an anglo woman; that woman doesn't have a Ph.D.; that woman failed in third grade.

We once thought that if we got educated it would lead to opportunity, and with opportunities we would find success, and then with success we would have power. But I beg you to stop that now, because that is not your indigenous way.

The real indigenous way is that you obtain knowledge, and knowledge helps you get wisdom, and with wisdom you grow strong, and with strength you find harmony. That is the paradigm that we should be reaching for, and not how many Ph.D's you can get, not how many books you can write, or how many books you can sell, or how many stories you can tell.

We've had to come through so many transitions, not just indigenous people on this side of the continent, indigenous people throughout the whole world. There is only one world, but all of these barriers have been put up to make us think that there's a third world, there's a second world, and we're in the first world.

The last time I saw Mother Earth there was only one world. What they're saying when they're talking about these worlds is just the exploitation of people and the degree that they are able to exploit people.

So I think that we have to make our way back to that indigenous path where we were all sisters and brothers, and when the sky and the earth were our elders and our parents were our leaders, and justice was the guide. Because we are lost now. Our aura has a hole in it, and we've got to balance ourselves, and we've got to close that hole in the aura of Mother Earth, and when we get that balance, and we know that justice is our guide, that aura, that hole around Mother Earth will close, and we will know that we are on the right path.

Amy Wong Mok

President, Texas Association Against Sexual Assault

Today, in 1996, we still have survivors who are required by some police officers in Texas to take a polygraph before police will take on their case. We still have survivors of sexual violence who have to show that they have black and blue marks on their bodies in order for some police officers to take on their case.

It is very sad that under Texas law, if you cannot show any forcible compulsion, then it is not rape. The words of women, when we say, "No," do not count.

Twenty years ago a group of radical people started talking in public about sexual violence against women in New York. That was our first "Take Back the Night" rally against sexual violence nationwide. In the same year another group of people in California started a 24-hour hotline for the survivors of rape.

Today I would like to pay tribute to those women who dare to blaze new trails, who dare to demand justice. Some will call them "radical feminists." Today we have more names to describe feminists; we have the "victim feminists"; we have the "feminazis" and so on, but all these names can only serve one purpose. That is to divide us. We must not pay attention to people who use our language to divide us.

I would like to share with you two Zen Buddhist teachings. Hopefully these will help us continue to do our work, because our work is very hard. The first teaching goes like this:

"To our past we must give our infinite appreciation, because many people have worked very hard to get where we are. To the present we must give our infinite appreciation, otherwise we will be in such despair that we cannot go on. To our future, we must give our infinite responsibility."

Another teaching goes like this:

"Only the reformers will see that this world is not perfect." I think we are all reformers, but we must unite. We must get together, gather our strength. We are not just our sister's and our brother's keeper, we are our brothers and our sisters. And I think that is what feminist values are about. Thank you.

What is the Foundation for a Compassionate Society?

by Genevieve Vaughan

Gen at the Nevada nuclear test site.

The Foundation for a Compassionate Society grew out of a theory of social change based on women's values. Ancient and modern mother-based cultures have distributed goods to the needy, maintaining both peace and abundance. Although it loudly advertises itself, patriarchy has notoriously failed in these areas. The cruel and needless starvation and death of millions, the unspeakable horror of ever more technologically advanced wars, the physical and psychological torture and rape of the vulnerable, the sex trafficking of millions of children and women, the concealed abuse and sex torture of children and women in the home, the exploitation and domination of nation upon nation, class upon class, race upon race, and finally the subjugation and consequent long term devastation of the environment and extinction of innumerable species, all bespeak the failure of patriarchy. The discrediting of the nurturing mother as the model of the human and her replacement by the competitive and hierarchical father is the basis of a duplicitous system which appears to provide for the many while actually placing them at the service of the few, turning the flow of goods away from the needs and towards the accumulation and luxury consumption of those with the cash. During the cold war, patriarchal capitalism and equally patriarchal communism wasted the wealth of the world on a struggle between 'brothers' to see which had the bigger 'weapon' and would therefore dominate.

Society cannot exist without mothers because free nurturing is necessary for the physical and psychological well being of humans. Free nurturing is the economic way basic to humans, by which they take care of needs. It has been excluded from narrowly defined 'economics' which requires a market and exchange. The 'free

Photos in this section are from the archives of the Foundatin for a Compassionate Society.

market' is the diametric opposite of 'free nurturing'. In fact 'free market' is an oxymoron. In the market nothing is free. Exchange—giving in order to receive an equivalent—competes with and overcomes free giving to satisfy needs. I believe we need to re-evaluate free nurturing, the mothering way towards which half of humanity is still socialized, and consider it the basis of economics. Exchange, which can be seen as a double gift, is usually considered the founding principle of economics. Could a single, one way need-satisfying gift then not be 'economic'?

Exchange has many defects which are not usually apparent to those who are practicing it. The logic of giving-in-order-to-receive transforms the other-oriented gift into an ego-oriented interaction. In exchange we concentrate on what we receive rather than on the need of the other person. The emphasis on the ego leads to domination which involves constraining others to 'freely' nurture the ego. This happens on many different levels. For example, profit—or what Karl Marx called 'surplus value'—can be seen in these terms as free gifts given by the many to the few. The workers nurture the capitalist. The low cost of labor and raw materials in the countries of the South create a situation in which despite protestations of benevolence on the part of the North, the South is actually nurturing the North, and is becoming depleted (underdeveloping) in the process.

Exchange requires scarcity in order to prevail as an economic logic, because if everyone lived in abundance, satisfying each others' needs, there would be no need to exchange, nor to have a market, nor a hierarchy of power and wealth. By making money through wasting the wealth of the world on armaments, drugs and other products which do not satisfy human needs, businesses and governments create the conditions of scarcity which are necessary for exchange, the free market economy and the domination of the many by the few.

In this paradoxical and dysfunctional situation the best solution would be for everyone to return to a mothering economy based on giving to satisfy needs, a gift economy. I believe that this is the promise of feminism, of the international women's movement. A World Women's Economic Order based on the re-evaluation of nurturing would produce a new psychology and a new politics, leading to peace and abundance for all.

I am a wealthy woman and I want to make public a secret of the wealthy. Most—though not all —of us are not happy and the ones who are, are usually happy in spite of being wealthy not because of it. I am not saying abundance is wrong in itself. In fact I think that belief is one of the great misperceptions of our time. (In fact if abundance is bad, why should we provide it to everyone?) What is very negative is the lack of compassion that accompanies exploitation or that results from having a lot while others have nothing. I have known too many wealthy people who have ruined their lives with drugs, alcohol and violence. The ones who do manage to feel pretty good about themselves are using their money for nurturing. They are giving it away. How could anyone be happy knowing they were even partly responsible for the suffering and death of millions and the devastation of the planet? The ego is a fragile social product and cannot be strong enough to take on the responsibility for the horrors that the system is perpetrating in order to reproduce itself. Like HAL, the computer in 2001, patriarchal capitalism tricks everyone and over-rewards a few of its adepts, in order to continue to run things its way, enlarging and empowering itself. The highest and best use of wealth at this time in history is to create radical social change in the system that produced it.

The economic system based on exchange appears to be all there is —Reality. It maintains this appearance and supports its domination as a paradigm or world view by diminishing the importance of the free nurturing labor. It parasitically draws upon that labor however, so that women (and many men) are actually 'freely' nurturing the system that oppresses everyone. The first step out of this complex situation is the restoration and re evaluation of the gift paradigm, giving it the dignity of which it has been robbed, as a key for the understanding of life at all levels. Patriarchy has many failsafes to keep us from recognizing the importance of giftgiving. It has relegated nurturing to the mother-child relation and discredited receiving as 'dependence.' Instead we need to re create our social institutions according to the gift mode and to recognize the creativity of receiving. Gifts which are not well used are valueless. The ideological campaign against giftgiving and receiving and against those who are socialized to act within the gift paradigm-women- makes free giving seem to have no place in the real world.

The Foundation for a Compassionate Society was founded with the idea of restoring the gift paradigm to its dignity as a viable social strategy while at the same time pointing out the defects of the exchange paradigm. In fact giftgiving has been a major theme in many pre-capitalist cultures but has only been seen through the eyes of patriarchal anthropologists as a sort of proto-exchange. Instead as the economic way based on mothering it is a necessary substratum of any society and could be the basis for a future world based on caring for rather than excluding, competing with and even slaughtering the Other. We have created an aberrant system by socializing our little boys into aggressive patriarchal behavior, telling them they are a different category, almost a different species, from their nurturing mothers. We have been convinced by purely physiological differences that we belong to different categories with different life expectations and agendas. We are giving more importance to categorization than to human needs. In fact patriarchy can be seen as a disease or a psychosis of categorization, quantification and measurement. The goal of life seems to be to have the 'most' — the translation into socio-economic terms of the physiological 'difference' of the male which relegated him to a category 'superior' to his nurturing mother.

Other physiological differences such as race or age are also made to be the bases for categories which try to demonstrate their greater 'value' by dominating the 'inferior' categories and making them give to them. The effect of this parasitism then becomes its justification, because those who are malnourished grow up smaller, more vulnerable to disease, physically different from the over-nourished dominator categories. Nurturing requires the inclusion of the Other, and the attention to needs at all levels. It is this logic that could be the basis of a feminist movement which goes beyond the boundaries and categories of race, class, age, nationality, with respect towards one another's needs and creativity and with common knowledge of the need to change the system which is oppressing us all. The

Foundation for a Compassionate Society is attempting to promote the giftgiving way by making women realize that it already exists as a life logic which they are practicing but do not consciously recognize and validate as viable.

Because giftgiving has been captured inside the family, the Foundation for a Compassionate Society has tried to practice it outside the family. The Foundation has given women on its staff a chance to nurture social change projects of many kinds, and to create alternative models. Because many people have not received free gifts since childhood, the Foundation has sponsored physical spaces, retreat centers, and buildings where peace and justice and feminist groups could hold retreats and meetings and has made office space available free or at a low cost. Some of these projects were in successful operation for several years, but then closed for a variety of reasons.

The Austin Women's Peace House was in existence from 1985-1992, The Living Well Healing Center from 1993-1996, the Grassroots Peace Organizations Building 1987-1996. Alma de Mujer retreat Center on Lake Travis has been in operation since 1987 under the care of Marsha Goméz and Esther Martinez. It has not closed but has recently been donated to the Indigenous Women's Network. The caregivers at all these spaces create change by nurturing the nurturers, validating the gift model. Receiving free gifts allows people to restore dignity to that model, and to begin to practice it themselves in a variety of ways. The donation fund of the Foundation for many years gave money to social change projects though it is now no longer functioning.

The point of all of this activity has not been charity, which has mitigated but never altered the structures of oppression, but to change those structures themselves and the values which hold them in place. Many projects of the Foundation have had to do with truth telling, which satisfies the need for information and for alternative points of view which people are not getting from the self-dealing, main stream media. Many national and international fact-finding delegations have been organized by the Foundation to travel to areas of conflict and oppression, many peace meetings have been organized between women from countries at war with one another.

The voices of those who are undergoing the experiences have been heard and transmitted. Not only do Foundation staff members create alternative media programs, but they also pass on their knowledge by teaching others.

In 1983, I came back to Texas from Italy where I had lived for twenty years, determined to use my resources for social change, putting the gift economy idea into practice. I began the donation program and opened a retreat center, Stonehaven Ranch, near San Marcos, which non-profit groups working for social change could use free or at low cost. In 1985, because I believed strongly in the importance of the international women's movement, I provided the resources for many women from the U.S. and other countries to attend the U.N. Decade for Women final conference in Nairobi, Kenya. I also funded and helped to organize the Peace Tent there, a center for free speech and dialogue among women from countries in conflict. After the Nairobi Conference I helped to initiate and maintain Peace Caravans which traveled in Europe, the Soviet Union and the U.S., disseminating the information gathered in Nairobi and spreading the spirit of the conference to women who had not been able to attend.

In 1987 I began the Foundation for a Compassionate Society to give an identifiable character to the initiatives I and my co workers had begun. As the staff of the organization grew, a community formed which was diverse as to race, class, sexual orientation, age and nationality. I sponsored and helped to create many ongoing projects which took place internationally as well as nationally and locally, and always with women's leadership.

The name 'Compassionate Society' means not that we consider ourselves experts in compassion but that we are trying to make the society itself more compassionate. For example, it is clear that the needs of future generations are not being met and indeed are made more extreme, by the degradation of the environment. The values which allow the profitable but irresponsible production and dumping of chemical and radioactive waste continue to place ever greater burdens upon those who cannot protest, whether they are unborn generations, people blighted by poverty and racism, or even the innumerable species of plants and animals whose genes are presently being altered and degraded by these poisons. It is important to change those profit-based values so that the society itself no longer rewards the behavior which leads to such extreme situations. By supporting women to speak out, to identify general social needs and find ways of satisfying them, the Foundation for a Compassionate Society supports the half of humanity whose voices have not been heard in the definition of the human condition, to rework that definition according to the values of care.

Among the projects that have been put into effect over the last ten years, there are many in feminist media. The Feminist International Radio Endeavor is a bilingual short wave radio program originating in Costa Rica providing a women's perspective for two hours daily. I began this program in 1991, and have continued to support it since then. It has been broadcasting daily now for more than five years on Radio for Peace International, under the direction of Puerto Rican María Suarez and Chilean Katarina Anfossi. Women's Access to Technological Resources is a center in Austin for video, radio, and computer networking, where groups of women receive media training free. Women's media activists Fern, Amanda Johnston and Felicia Hayes coordinate trainings, do networking and work with volunteers in the production of special events. A day-long radio festival was held on International Women's Day 1996, in conjunction with community groups, local radio stations and Austin Community Television. Because of the success of that festival, Foundation and community members are planning to make it an annual event. The Foundation for a Compassionate Society provides ongoing support for Women's International Newsgathering Service (WINGS), a syndicated radio program now based in Austin, produced by Frieda Werden. The foundation staff also produce many community television shows which try to identify a socially compassionate perspective as well as providing information on women's issues and activities from the local to the global. The TV shows are produced with technical support from Beth Wichterich and women's spirituality activist, Pat Cuney.

Foundation staff members traveled to the Fourth World Women's Congress in Beijing and the NGO conference in Huairou (1995).

Upon our return we gave numerous community presentations in Austin and in surrounding areas. As follow-up to the Conference, the Foundation initiated a series of feminist gatherings and public presentations. The strong anti-nuclear sentiment of the international women's movement evidenced in Huairou was brought forward in a Feminist Anti-Nuclear Gathering at the end of March at Stonehaven Ranch, in which women activists from Europe and the Pacific came together with indigenous and non-indigenous women working in the anti-nuclear movement in the U.S..

The second conference in the Post-Beijing series was the public forum on Feminist Family Values held at the Austin Convention Center in May, which is the subject of this book. Angela Davis, Gloria Steinem, immigration activist María Jiménez, and Hawai'ian Land Rights activist Mililani Trask, gave alternative perspectives regarding issues which are usually considered patriarchal territory, to an enthusiastic crowd of 2000 feminists. Videos of this event and of the enlightening community panel which preceded it are now available. A conference is being planned for October on another theme which was much discussed in China: Right wing Fundamentalism. At this writing Robin Morgan, Mahnaz Afgami (Iran), and Yvonne Deutsch (Israel) have agreed to speak at this event. Other feminists and local activists from different religious and national backgrounds have been invited to address this burning issue. Still another forum, on the theme of Feminist Economics will be held in January with the help of Peruvian sociologist, Cristina Herencia.

Other ongoing projects of the Foundation and its more political aspect, Feminists for a Compassionate Society are: the Earth and Sky Women's Peace Caravan for a Nuclear Free Future through which Susan Lee, Erin Rogers and other staff and volunteers explain the dangers of nuclear production, transportation and dumping, especially in relation to the proposed nuclear dump in Sierra Blanca, Texas.

Health surveys regarding the effects of hazardous and toxic materials dumped on military bases in San Antonio, are being carried out by environmental caregivers Yana Bland and Carol Stall. The women are finding commonalities with similar problems in other regions of the world, such as the Phillipines. Yana, who is originally from Malta, is the founder of the Association of Women of the Mediterranean Region, which I have supported and which recently held its fifth annual meeting, on the island of Cyprus.

In 1992 I bought a piece of land near the nuclear test site in Nevada and with the help of many women built there a temple to the Egyptian goddess Sekhmet, the goddess of fertility and rage. This small straw bale and stucco construction is a sacred meditation space offered to all those who need to reinforce their hearts in the protest against the violence of technology, and the devastation caused by the nuclear cycle. It is a place to take a stand for the integrity of our genes and for the protection of Mother Earth against the violent penetration of underground nuclear testing. Ceremonies are held their under the guidance of spiritual caregiver Patricia Pearlman. Statues of Sekhmet and of Mother Earth were created by indigenous sculptor Marsha Goméz. Since the temple is a small structure, and does not take up much space, I decided to give back the land itself to the Western Shoshone, to whom all the nuclear test site area originally belonged. That restoration of property took place in 1992.

Other foundation projects include the retreat center Stonehaven Ranch, near San Marcos, Texas, which provides free or low cost space to groups working on feminist, peace and justice, and spirituality issues. Managed by Margie First, this lovely hill country ranch has housed literally thousands of activists since its inception in 1984. A resource center and museum for the indigenous peoples of the Americas, Casa de Colores, is located on the border between Texas and Mexico, near Brownsville, and is managed by Helga Garcia-Garza. Chicana land rights activist and midwife, Patti Salas gives her energy to projects regarding the environment and health. Poet María Limón works on environmental and Chicana issues and produces the Foundation newsletter. Performance artist Sally Jacques works on special projects, among which the Austin-to-Bosnia material aid project was particularly significant. Environmentalist Suze Kemper provides technical assistance and Sue MacNichols provides backup and networking for many of the Foundation projects. San Juanita Alcala and Rosa Corrales provide administrative support. There have been ongoing projects for many years in both Europe and South America.

All of the projects I have described and many others have been an attempt to emphasize the importance of the values of care. In other words they are an attempt to put into practice a kind of meta-funding, a giving about giving. They have been an attempt to use money to fund non-monetary values, values which are beyond exchange itself, and beyond domination and ego orientation. My belief is that by giving value to these values a ripple effect will occur, they will begin to come forward in everyone's consciousness, and people will begin to act accordingly. We will cease rewarding personal, economic, and military aggression and will begin rewarding the behavior which satisfies needs, at all levels (material, psychological, social etc.).

The women of the Foundation for a Compassionate Society invite the collaboration and input of the public so that we may all work together towards a better world based upon the mothering values of care. We invite you to add your contribution to the monetary needs of these projects as well to volunteer the time and energy it takes to get work done so that we can continue to practice these values in socially significant ways, to change the system of patriarchy which is presently making life impossible on our beautiful Mother Earth.

Write to: Foundation for a Compassionate Society, PO Box 868, Kyle, Texas, 78640.

Editor's Note: The photographs on the following pages are part of the Foundation archives. They present a sample of Foundation projects, facilities and workers.

International Special Projects
Sponsored by the
Foundation for a Compassionate Society

Meeting with COMADRES, Mothers of the Disappeared of El Salvador in 1984.

Women at the Peace Tent, Nairobi, 1985. UN Decade for Women Final Conference.

Women at the Peace Tent, Nairobi, 1985. UN Decade for Women Final Conference.

Delegation of US women to an international women's meeting in Cuba.

Fact finding trip to Central America with Attorney Generals from various US states.

Women for Meaningful Summits meeting at Stonehaven, 1990.

Indigenous Women's Tour of Europe, Rome, 1993.

Ellen Diederich, 4-Directions Store, Germany,
Founder Peace Archives, Oberhauser, Germany

Association of Women of the Mediterranean Region, 5th annual conference, June 1996.

Association of Women of the Mediterranean Region at the temple of the goddess in Malta.

Community meeting at cultural museum, Casa de Colores, Brownsville, TX. Casa de Colores deals with border issues between Mexico and the U.S.

4th Annual U.N. Conference on Women, Beijing, China, 1995.

Austin to Bosnia Project (directed by Sally Jacques) exhibit in Beijing. Project collected food, clothing and medical supplies and sent them to Bosnia during the war.
Photos by Sally Jacques.

Facilities
Sponsored by the
Foundation for a Compassionate Society

Grassroots Peace Organizations Building, Austin, TX 1987-1996.

4-Directions Store, Oberhausen, Germany.

Stonehaven Ranch, retreat and conference center, Central Texas. Photo © Jane Steig Parsons, Prints Charming Photography

Conference group at Stonehaven Ranch.

WATER (Women's Access to Electronic Resources).

Margie First, manager along with Paméla Overynder of Stonehaven Ranch.

Alma de Mujer, conference retreat center. Donated in 1996 to the Indigenous Women's Network.

127

Media Projects
Sponsored by the
Foundation for a Compassionate Society

FIRE: Katarina Anjossi.

FIRE (Feminist International Radio
Endeavor), Costa Rica. Front row:
Genevieve Vaughan, Delora Latham (Radio
for Peace International), Sally Jacques; Back
Row: Katarina Anjossi, María Suarez.

Frieda Werden: WINGS
(Women's International
News Gathering
Service)

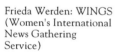

Frieda Werden interviewing Bella Abzug for WINGS.

Gloria Steinem at WATER (Women's Access to Electronic Resources).

Trella Laughlan,
Video Producer,
Public Access
television program,
"Speak Out."

Training session at WATER.

Anti-Nuclear Projects
Sponsored by the
Foundation for a Compassionate Society

Demonstration at Pantex, Amarillo, TX, 1985. We had a replica of the Nairobi Peace tent made and have used it many places since.

Blessing of the land bordering the nuclear test site in Nevada 1992.

Temple to the Egyptian Goddess Sekhmet, Cactus Springs, Nevada. Cynthia Burkhardt and

Someof the women of the affinity group, led by Paméla Overynder, which built the straw bale temple in Nevada.

Genevieve Vaughan, March 1996. FANG (Feminist Anti-Nuclear Gathering—held at Stonehaven Ranch) press conference.

March of children from Acuma, Mexico protesting at the Texas Governor's Mansion, the proposed nuclear waste dump in Sierra Blanca, Texas. June 5, 1996.

Women's Peace Caravan (led by Susan Lee) at public hearing about the proposed nuclear waste dump, Sierra Blanca, TX August 7-8, 1996.